Collins

Perfect Maths 2

Prabha Sethy

Components of DigiSuite

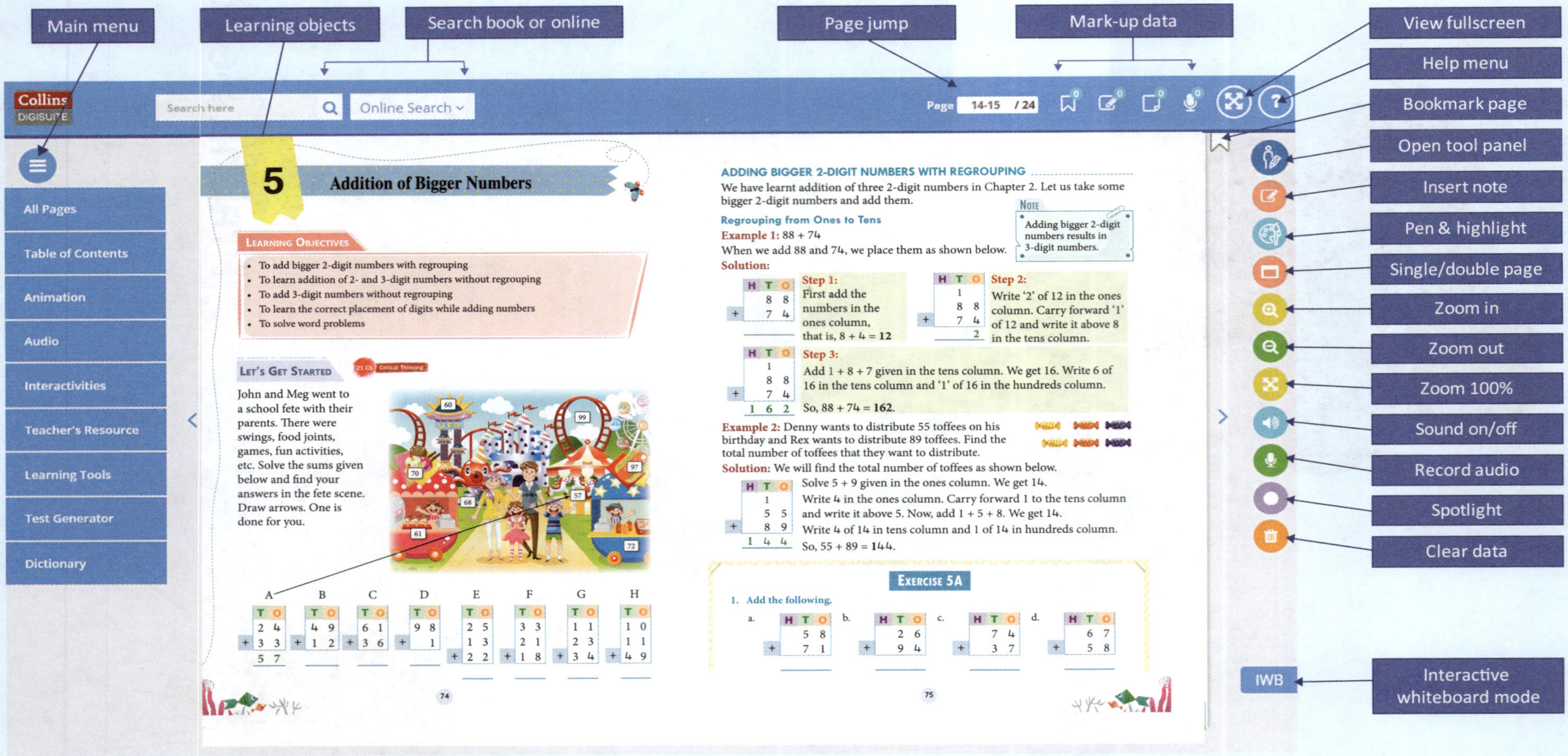

Student + Teacher			Teacher-only	
a animations	**ia** activities	**g** games	**lp** lesson plans	**tn** teacher's notes
ilt instructor-led tutorials	**w** worksheets	**v** videos	**w** worksheets	**ak** answer keys
	audio			

Preface

Perfect Maths is a series of eleven books for Classes Nursery to 8. The books for the Foundational Stage, previously referred to as Grades Nursery, Lower KG and Upper KG, would be the base to make the series complete in providing a strong foundation in numeracy, starting from ECCE till the middle stage. The series adheres to the guidelines of the **National Education Policy (NEP) 2020**, aligns with the vision of the ***National Initiative for Proficiency in Reading with Understanding and Numeracy*** **(NIPUN Bharat)** and aims to make mathematics more relevant to students in a non-threatening way.

The books for Foundational Stage 1 to 3 (Grades Nursery to UKG) are focused on the holistic development of a child. Based on **Numeracy Skills**, **21st Century Skills** and **Multiple Intelligences**, integrated and interdisciplinary approach, experiential learning, the books aim to help a child be "**Happy to Learn**". The unique blend of direct instructions, play-based structured activities, investigations, stories and rhymes provide the children ample opportunities to develop their numeracy and literacy skills.

The books for Classes 1 to 8 follow the ***5E Learning Model***. The 5E Learning Model provides an activity-oriented approach to the series to make mathematics engaging for students through emphasizing connections between mathematics and day-to-day experiences. This series adheres to the guidelines of NEP 2020 completely, with the effective integration of its features with **21st Century Skills**, **Art Integration**, **Experiential Learning**, **Cross-curricular** and **India Focus**. The skill building questions and the varied exposure to situations provided in the pages of this series keep the learners at the centre and focus on making them future-ready. The series also aims to make students aware of the United Nations **Sustainable Development Goals** (SDGs), so that they can become SDG Pioneers, Champions or Ambassadors.

SAFAL in ***Perfect Maths:*** This series also strives to make a shift from rote-learning to competency-based learning, in accordance with **Structured Assessment For Analyzing Learning (SAFAL)**. The components of SAFAL—critical thinking, inquiry-based learning and analysis-based learning—are woven into the features such as Exercises, Mental Maths, Chapter Revision, Skill Up!, Worksheets, Reasoning Worksheets, Review/Assessment Corner and PISA Corner (Classes 6 to 8).

We would like to take this opportunity to thank all the teachers and educationist who reviewed the books and provided their feedback, which helped in improving the quality of the content.

Feedback, invaluable comments and suggestions from users are welcome.

Authors

About the Author

Prabha Sethy, formerly a teacher at Welham Boys' School, Dehradun, with more than 30 years of experience in teaching mathematics, brings in resources from everyday life into her content.

Key Features

The key features of ***Perfect Maths*** are completely aligned with the **National Education Policy (NEP) 2020** and the vision of the ***National Initiative for Proficiency in Reading with Understanding and Numeracy* (NIPUN Bharat)**. These meticulously designed features, based on the ***5E Learning Model***, can be used as learning strategies to enhance the understanding of key concepts in mathematics and increase practical learning and problem-solving by bringing in real-life contexts from outside the classroom while providing some form of experiential learning. These key features also aim to help the learners shift from rote-learning to competency-based learning, in accordance with ***Structured Assessment For Analyzing Learning*** (SAFAL).

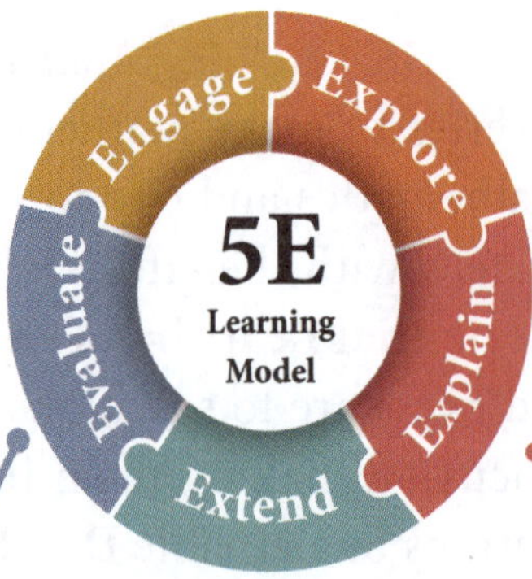

Engage: To capture the attention of students, get them mentally engaged and make connections between past and present

- Maths Around Us
- Let's Get Started
- Common Errors
- Go Easy!
- Vedic Maths (Classes 6 to 8)
- Eminent Mathematicians
- Poster

Explore: To enable the students to explore the concepts through hands-on activities, investigations, etc.

- Maths Lab Activity
- Crosswords
- Puzzles
- Mental Maths
- Worksheets
- Maths Mela

Explain: To enable the students to understand the main ideas of the topics

- Learning Objectives
- Note
- Solved Examples
- Concept Map
- Key Concepts

Extend: To enable the students to stimulate thinking and apply prior and current knowledge to real-life situations

- Do You Know?
- Word Problems
- Skill Up!
- SEE Learning

Evaluate: To review, assess and evaluate what students have learned

- Exercises
- Chapter Revision
- Reasoning Worksheet
- Review/Assessment Corner
- PISA Corner (Classes 6 to 8)

Adherence to National Education Policy

21st Century Skills (21 CS)

Learning Skills
- Critical Thinking
- Creativity and Innovation
- Collaboration
- Communication

Life Skills

Literacy Skills
- Information Literacy
- Media Literacy
- Technology Literacy

Art Integration (AI)

Cross Curricular (CC)

India Focus (IF)

Happiness Quotient (HQ)

Experiential Learning (EL)

SUSTAINABLE DEVELOPMENT GOALS

Each feature has been tagged with colour-coded icons to easily identify the type of skills and learning being addressed!

About the Features

Interesting information and activities to connect maths with Indian history, art, culture, real-life situations and financial literacy

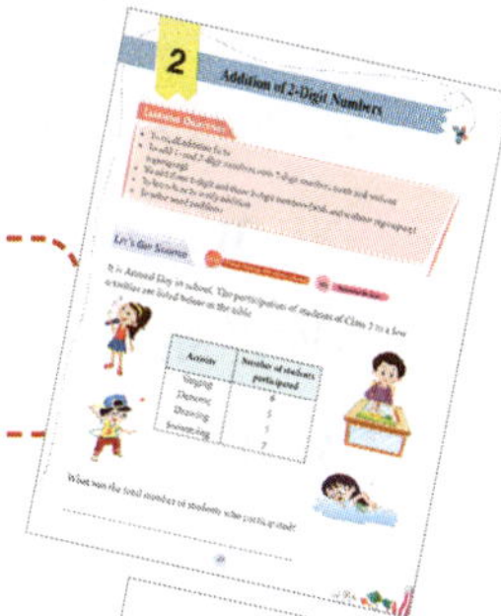

Chapter starter in the form of a picture-based exercise

Hands-on activity to help in improving investigation, reinforcement and extension of concepts just learnt

A variety of questions catering to inquiry-based, discovery-based, discussion-based and analysis-based learning

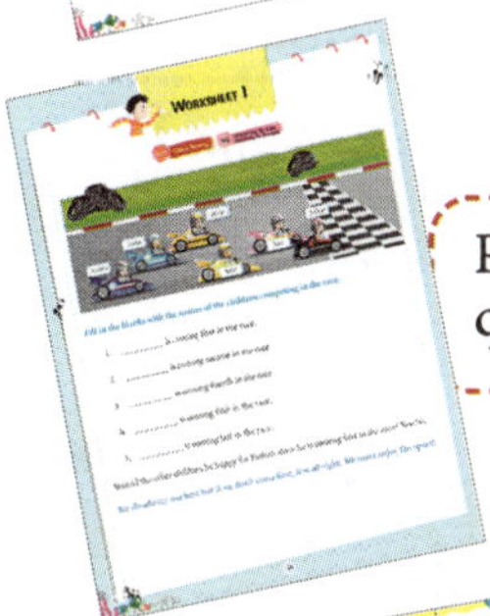

Picture-based, fun, problem-solving questions to reinforce concepts

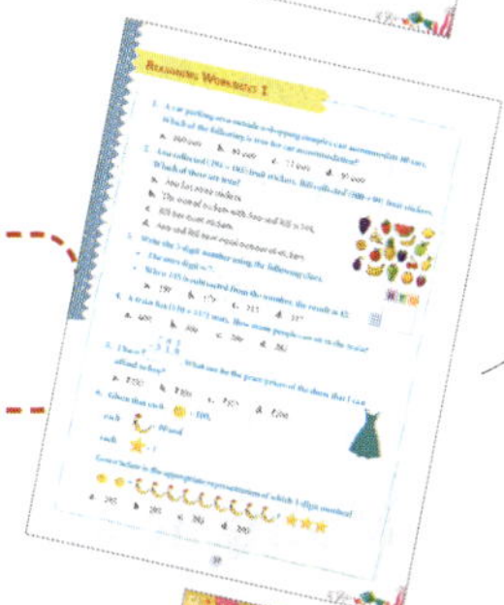

Questions to stimulate rational thinking using mathematical skills

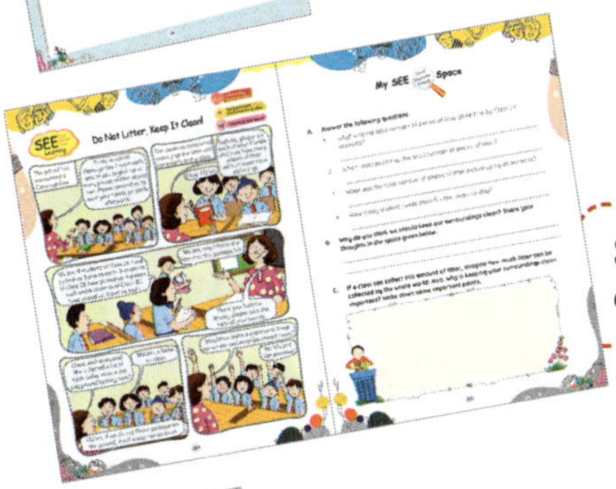

Special stories to promote social, emotional and ethical learning

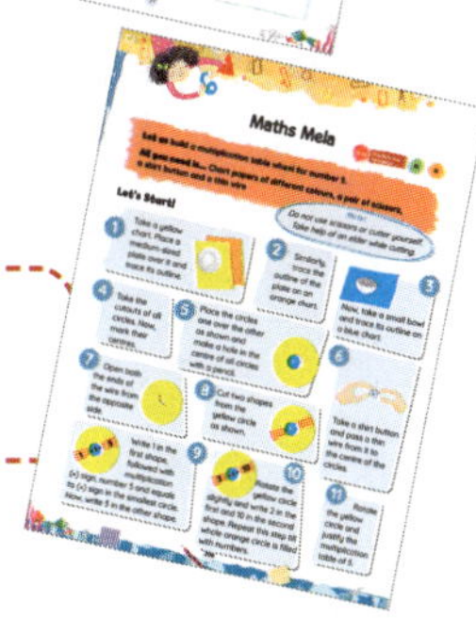

Model making or hands-on project ideas to enhance learning beyond the classroom

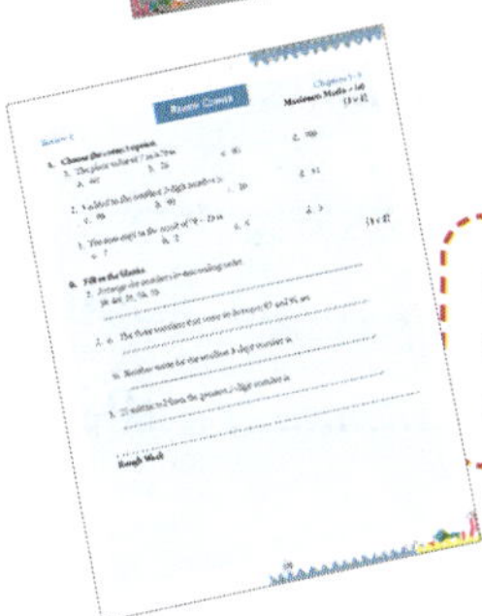

Sample test papers at the end of the book for additional practice (Classes 6 to 8 Assessment Corner based on the **New Assessment format**)

Brief write-ups on eminent mathematicians and their contributions

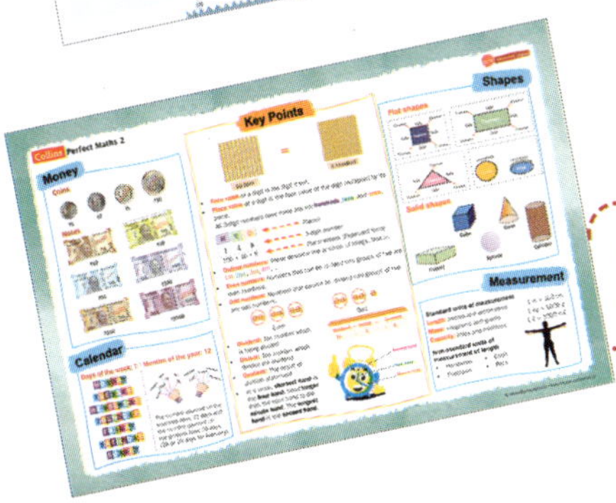

Informative colourful posters to focus on some important concepts or facts

Contents

Maths Around Us

21 CS Information Literacy | CC Integration with Environmental Studies

COLOURS, SHAPES AND PATTERNS OF LEAVES

Do you know that by looking at the colour of some leaves, we can identify the season?

Here are some leaves that change colour across different seasons in a year. Maple and birch are such trees whose leaves change colour from one season to another.

Maple trees look the most beautiful in autumn. In spring, the leaves are reddish in colour. In summer, the leaves are usually green. In autumn, the colour of the leaves changes to many shades of orange, yellow and brown.

Do you know which country's flag has maple leaf as a symbol?

You can also observe different patterns in leaves.

Look around your neighbourhood or locality. Are there any trees whose leaves change colour across different seasons? Collect such leaves and paste in the space provided below. Write a few lines about the colour and the pattern of the leaves.

Paste the leaves here.

1 Numbers up to 200

Learning Objectives

- To read, write and compare numbers up to 200 and write their number names
- To understand face value, place value and expanded form
- To learn the ordering of numbers
- To understand what are even/odd numbers and learn about ordinal numbers

Let's Get Started

21 CS Critical Thinking

1. Write the numbers given below in descending order inside the balloons. (left to right)   98,   45,   23,   67,   12
2. Write the numbers and the number names corresponding to pink, purple, blue and green balloons.

   a. _____ = ________________   b. _____ = ________________

   c. _____ = ________________   d. _____ = ________________
3. The balloon with the smallest number is ________ in colour.
4. The balloon with the greatest number is ________ in colour.
5. The blue balloon is placed just after the ________ balloon.
6. The orange balloon is placed just before the ________ balloon.
7. Compare the numbers in green and pink balloons using > or <.

   ________ ☐ ________
8. Blue balloon is in between ________ and ________ balloons.

INTRODUCTION TO NUMBERS UP TO 200

We have learnt the numbers from 1 to 99 in the previous class.

When 1 is added to 99, we get a 3-digit number, that is, 100.

$$99 + 1 = 100$$

The two zeros are written under Ones and Tens and 1 is written under Hundreds.

We can write it as:

Hundreds	Tens	Ones
H	T	O
1	0	0

NOTE

100 is the smallest 3-digit number.

Numbers from 101 to 200

Let us have a look at the 3-digit numbers from 101 to 200.

101	102	103	104	105	106	107	108	109	110
111	112	113	114	115	116	117	118	119	120
121	122	123	124	125	126	127	128	129	130
131	132	133	134	135	136	137	138	139	140
141	142	143	144	145	146	147	148	149	150
151	152	153	154	155	156	157	158	159	160
161	162	163	164	165	166	167	168	169	170
171	172	173	174	175	176	177	178	179	180
181	182	183	184	185	186	187	188	189	190
191	192	193	194	195	196	197	198	199	200

GO EASY!

Word form of a number is the same as its number name. Short form of the word form is the numeral itself.

NOTE

Each number given inside this grid is 1 more than its previous number.

Nick loves to eat cookies. He buys at least 2 to 3 packs of cookies each time he visits the market. One pack contains 10 cookies. Let us see how many cookies he bought.

1 packet = 10 cookies. How many cookies will there be in 10 such packets?

Using repeated addition, we must add 10, ten times.

10 + 10 + 10 + 10 + 10 + 10 + 10 + 10 + 10 + 10 = **100 cookies**

100 cookies can be shown as,

The two zeros are written under Ones and Tens columns and 1 is written under Hundreds column.

He also bought 1 loose cookie, so to find the answer, we add 100 and 1.

	H	T	O
	1	0	0
+			1
	1	**0**	**1**

cookies

So, Nick purchased **101** cookies. It is read as '**one hundred one**'. This number can be represented using cookies as,

= **101**

1 hundred

1 one

Number name of 101 = One hundred one

Let us learn more about 3-digit numbers.

While reading a 3-digit number, the number formed by the digits at tens and ones places is read and spoken together.

For example, 156 is read as one hundred **fifty-six**.

Now, consider the following set of cookies.

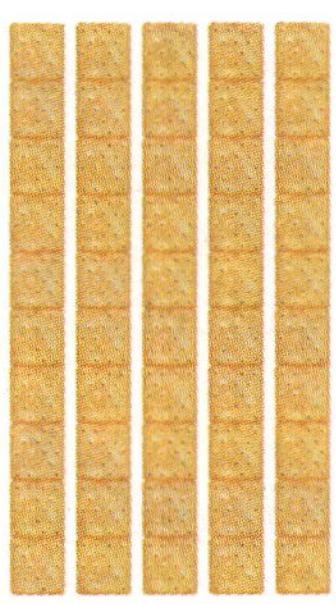

=

H	T	O
1	5	6

1 hundred

5 tens

6 ones

Number name of 156
= One hundred fifty-six

Let us understand the number 200 by considering the following sets of cookies.

The number 200 comes just after 199. So, it will have 2 sets of hundred cookies.

2 hundreds

=

H	T	O
2	0	0

Number name of 200
= Two hundred

Similarly, we can also read and write other 3-digit numbers like 102, 103, 104, 111, 112, 132, 144, 147, 161, 179 and so on.

NOTE

Predecessor is the number just before a given number.

Example: 123 is predecessor of 124.

Successor is the number just after a given number.

Example: 192 is successor of 191.

DO YOU KNOW?

Harriet is a tortoise that lived for 175 years. It belonged to the species of Galapagos Tortoise. It was last found in Queensland, Australia.

As we observed, 175 is a 3-digit number. Can you call aloud its number name?

EXERCISE 1A

1. Fill in the blanks.

a. 

Hundreds Ones

Hundreds H	Tens T	Ones O

Number name = ____________

b. 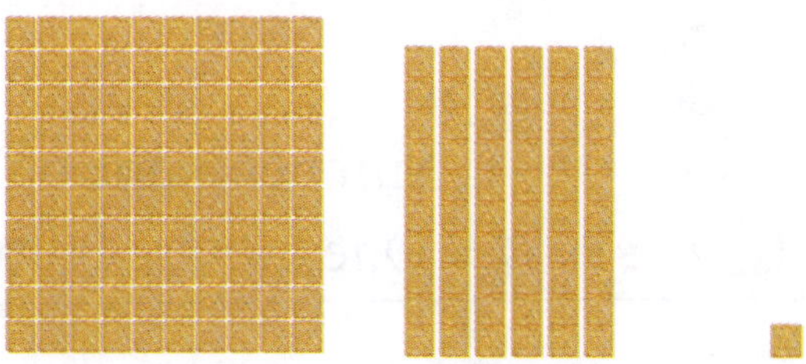

Hundreds Tens Ones

Hundreds H	Tens T	Ones O

Number name = ____________

2. **Write the numeral for each number name.**

a. One hundred seventy [ ]   b. One hundred eighty-seven [ ]

3. **Write the number name for each numeral.**

a. 143 = ______________________________

b. 155 = ______________________________

4. **Match the following.**

Column A / **Column B**

	H	T	O	**Number Names**
a.	1	3	5	One hundred
b.	1	0	3	One hundred three
c.	1	0	0	One hundred forty-eight
d.	1	4	8	One hundred seventy-six
e.	1	7	6	One hundred thirty-five

5. **Complete the grid from 151 to 200. Call aloud the number names.**

151									
	162							169	
				175	176				
181									190
			194			197			200

6. **Write the numbers just after:**

a. 161 [ ]   b. 196 [ ]

7. **Write the numbers just before:**

a. [ ] 200   b. [ ] 127

8. **Complete the pattern.** 191, 190, [ ], [ ], [ ], [ ]

9. **What is the predecessor of 167?** [ ]

10. **What is the successor of 110?** [ ]

FACE VALUE AND PLACE VALUE

Each digit in a number has a face value and a place value.

Face value of a digit is the digit itself.

Place value of a digit is the face value of the digit multiplied by its place.

This shows the relationship between face value and place value.

> **NOTE**
>
> **Face value** of a digit cannot be changed.
>
> **Place value** of a digit can be changed. It depends on the place of the digit in the number.
>
> **Example:** Consider the numbers, 135 and 153.
>
> - Face value of 3 in both 135 and 153 is 3.
> - Place value of 3 in 135 is 30 and place value of 3 in 153 is 3.

A 1-digit number has one digit, placed at the ones place.

Example 1: Consider the number 5. Face value of 5 is 5. Place value of 5 is 5.

A 2-digit number has two digits. The first digit of the number from its right is placed under the ones place and the other digit is placed under the tens place.

For example, in number 25, 5 is placed under ones place and 2 is placed under tens place.

Tens	Ones
2	5

Digits in the number 25	Face value	Place value
2	2	20
5	5	5

A 3-digit number has three digits. The first digit of the number from its right is placed under the ones place, the second digit is placed under the tens place and the last digit is placed under the hundreds place.

For example, in number 152, 2 is placed under ones place, 5 is placed under tens place and 1 is placed under hundreds place.

Hundreds	Tens	Ones
1	5	2

Digits in the number 152	Face value	Place value
1	1	100
5	5	50
2	2	2

EXPANDED FORM

The expanded form of a number is written as an addition statement of the place values of all the digits. Consider the place values of the digits of the number 148 in the given table.

Digits in the number 148	Place value	Expanded form
1	100	100 + 40 + 8 or 1 hundred + 4 tens + 8 ones
4	40	
8	8	

EXERCISE 1B

1. **Write the face value and place value of the coloured digits.**

   a. 107

   Face value: ____________

   Place value: ____________

   b. 187

   Face value: ____________

   Place value: ____________

2. **Write the expanded form of each number.**

   a. 150 = ________________________________

   b. 100 = ________________________________

   c. 141 = ________________________________

   d. 113 = ________________________________

3. **Write the numbers corresponding to the given expanded forms.**

   a. 1 hundred + 9 ones = [ ]

   b. 100 + 60 + 7 = [ ]

   c. 100 + 5 = [ ]

   d. 1 hundred + 2 tens + 3 ones = [ ]

4. **Given below is a representation of 100 cookies, 10 cookies and 1 cookie.**

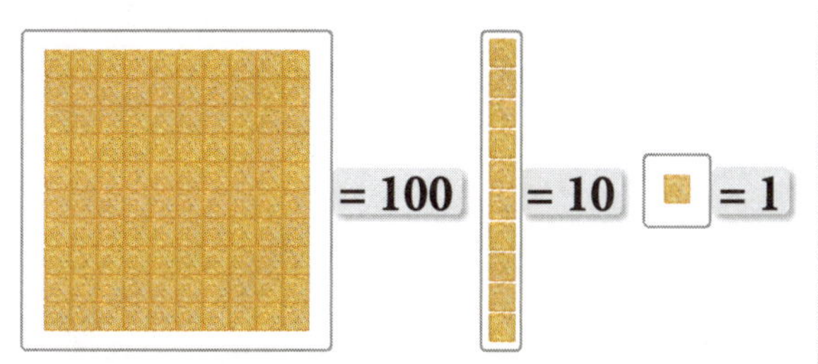

Write the expanded form of the following as per the given representation.

a.

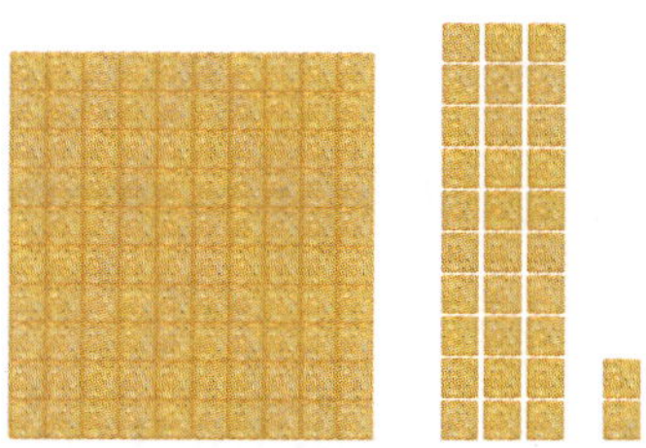

b.

NUMBER COMPARISON

We have learnt about less than, greater than and equals to symbols in Class 1.

Symbol for Less than is **$<$**

Symbol for Greater than is **$>$**

Symbol for Equals to is **$=$**

When we compare two numbers, we find out whether a number is greater than or less than or equal to another number.

Comparing a 3-Digit and a 2-Digit Number

Compare 193 and 99.

The number with lesser number of digits is smaller.

So, $99 < 193$ or $193 > 99$.

Comparing Two 2-Digit Numbers

Compare 57 and 75.

Compare the digits in the tens place. 5 is less than 7.

So, $57 < 75$ or $75 > 57$.

If the Digits at the Tens Place are Same, then Compare the Digits at the Ones Place.

If we compare 68 and 61, we observe that 6 occurs at the tens place in both the numbers. Then, comparing the ones digits, we find that 8 is greater than 1. Hence, 68 is greater than 61.

Comparing Two 3-Digit Numbers

Compare 153 and 127.

Steps:

1. First, compare the digits in the hundreds place. Both the numbers have 1 in the hundreds place, so move to the next step.
2. Now, compare the digits in the tens place. We find that 5 is greater than 2. So, $153 > 127$.

- If the digits at both the hundreds and tens places are equal, then compare the digits at the ones place. For example, compare 139 and 134. Here, 1 and 3 occur at the hundreds and tens places, respectively, in both the numbers. Comparing the digits at the ones place, we find that 9 is greater than 4.

  So, $139 > 134$.

Mental Maths

1. Write the numeral for one hundred eleven. ____________
2. Write the number name of 184. ________________________________
3. Write the face value and the place value of 9 in 149. ____________, ____________
4. Write the number that comes just before 149. ____________
5. Write the expanded form of 116. ______________

Exercise 1C

1. Tick (✓) the greater number.

a. 135 ☐ 133 ☐ b. 200 ☐ 172 ☐

c. 111 ☐ 100 ☐ d. 165 ☐ 156 ☐

2. Circle the smallest number.

a. 133 122 111 b. 111 109 191

c. 122 169 154 d. 151 180 116

3. Compare the numbers using >, < or =.

a. 175 ☐ 185 b. 146 ☐ 144 c. 198 ☐ 200 d. 153 ☐ 153

4. Colour the greatest number.

a. 144 134 194 b. 107 108 105

c. 147 144 142 d. 161 188 195

ORDERING OF NUMBERS

The teacher in a classroom placed five paper chits on her table. She wrote down 5 random numbers on these 5 chits. Then she asked 5 students to pick up the chits without looking at them.

Nick, Roma, Kavya, Radhika and Sam picked up the chits and the numbers written on them are shown in the picture on the following page.

They are standing in order of the numbers from smallest to the greatest. This shows that they are standing in **increasing or ascending order** of the numbers picked by them. That is, 17, 95, 137, 160, 199.

However, when they stand from right to left, that is Sam, Radhika, Kavya, Roma and Nick, the order of numbers becomes greatest to smallest. This is known as the **decreasing or descending order**.

That is, 199, 160, 137, 95, 17.

EXERCISE 1D

1. Arrange the following numbers in ascending order.

a. 130, 10, 155, 166, 110, 190 ____________________

b. 111, 151, 189, 107, 170, 45 ____________________

2. Arrange the following numbers in descending order.

a. 199, 200, 191, 198, 192, 195 ____________________

b. 188, 108, 118, 181, 110, 106 ____________________

ORDINAL NUMBERS

Ordinal numbers help us to understand the position of objects. We use the following terms: First for 1, Second for 2, Third for 3 and so on.

Ordinal numbers from 1 to 10 are given below.

Position:	1	2	3	4	5
Ordinal:	First	Second	Third	Fourth	Fifth
Written as:	1st	2nd	3rd	4th	5th

Position:	6	7	8	9	10
Ordinal:	Sixth	Seventh	Eighth	Ninth	Tenth
Written as:	6th	7th	8th	9th	10th

EXERCISE 1E

1. Before going for a birthday party, Sunny placed his outfit to wear on the bed in a sequence. The sequence is given below.

Answer the following.

a.  is the ____________ (first/third) item placed on the bed.

b. The _______ (second/third) item he wore, were his  .

c. It was winter season. So, Sunny picked up the ____________ (second/fifth) item to wear.

d. Which item did he wear around his neck? It is the ____________ (third/fourth) item in the sequence.

e. He wishes to wear the trousers in the end. State true or false. ____________

f. He has placed the trousers at the ____________ (first/second) position.

2. There are 26 letters in English alphabet. The first 10 letters are given below.

A B C D E F G H I J

a. Which is the second letter? ____________

b. G comes just after F. G is the ____________ letter. (sixth/seventh)

c. Write the tenth letter ____________. Which letter is just before the tenth letter? ____________

d. Name and write the colour of the fifth letter. ____________

e. C comes in between ____________ and ____________. The letter C is at the ____________ position. (third/fifth)

EVEN AND ODD NUMBERS

What are **pairs of objects**?

One Pair = 2 Objects

When two objects are placed together, they are considered as one pair.

Consider the following objects around you that occur in pairs.

a pair of shoes

a pair of socks

a pair of gloves

a pair of earrings

This shows that things that occur in **pairs** are basically **groups of two objects.**

We also have pairs of organs in our body like 2 eyes, 2 ears, 2 hands, 2 legs, 2 feet, 2 arms, 2 lungs, etc.

Consider a pair of earrings.

One pair has **2** earrings.

Now consider, two pairs of earrings.

Two pairs have 4 earrings.

Three pairs of earrings are shown below.

Three pairs have **6** earrings.

Four pairs of earrings are shown below.

Four pairs have **8** earrings.

Five pairs of earrings are shown below.

Five pairs have **10** earrings.

Numbers that can be divided into groups of two are **even numbers**. An **even number** is a number whose last digit is 0, 2, 4, 6 or 8.
Examples: 32, 54, 126, 178, 190

Numbers that cannot be divided into groups of two are **odd numbers**. An **odd number** is a number whose last digit is 1, 3, 5, 7 or 9.
Examples: 21, 63, 145, 187, 199

Common Errors

1. 012 👎 120 👍
   A number cannot start with 0.
2. Ordinal numbers:
   4th = Forth 👎 Fourth 👍
   9th = Nineth 👎 Ninth 👍
3. Number names:
   40
   Fourty 👎 Forty 👍
   19
   Ninteen 👎 Nineteen 👍

Exercise 1F

1. Out of the numbers given below, write all the even numbers in House A and all the odd numbers in House B.

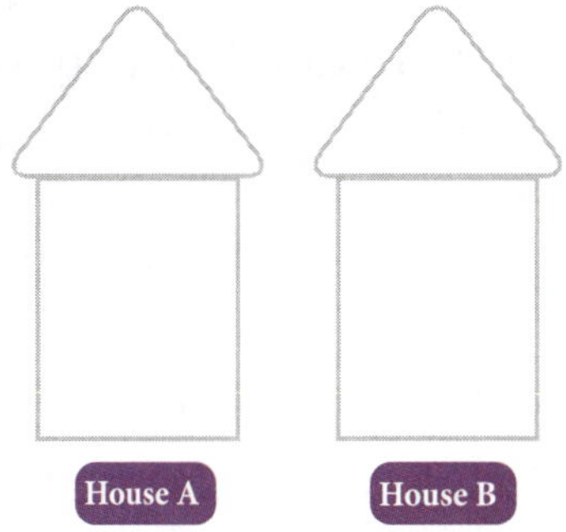

125 21 150 142 4 160 194 161

2. Group the following shapes by circling them in pairs. Count the total and check whether it is even or odd. One has been done for you.

a. 

b. 

c. 

d.

e. 

f. 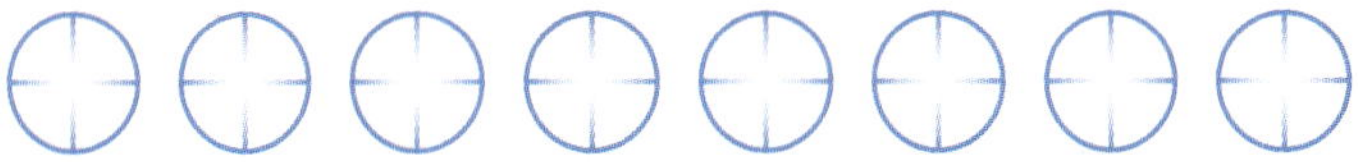

Number	Even/Odd
5	Odd

3. Circle the objects that occur in pairs.

Mental Maths

1. Both Kanu and Renu have 1 rupee coins. Kanu has 110 coins and Renu has 125 coins. Who has more money? ________
2. Fill in the blanks.
   a. 145 is __________ than 140. b. 190 is __________ than 191.
3. Write T for true and F for false.
   a. 124 > 170 __________
   b. One hundred eleven is the word form of 111. __________
   c. 199 is an even number. __________
   d. The place value of 1 in 132 is 10. __________

MATHS LAB ACTIVITY

21 CS Critical Thinking, Collaboration EL

Aim: To develop an understanding of numbers, number names and expanded form of numbers up to 200

Materials required: Pen, notebook

Procedure:

1. Conduct an activity by assigning numbers from 1 to 9 each to nine different students.
2. Let each of the remaining other students be assigned the number 10.
3. The teacher calls out the number, 48. The students gather together as shown below.

10 10 10 10 8

4 students with the number 10 and 1 student with the number 8 gather together.

= 48

4. Similarly, try forming other numbers, such as 125, as shown below.

10 10 10 10 10 10 10 10 10 10 = 100

10 10 = 20

5 = 5

Adding 100, 20 and 5, we get 125.

5. Now, the teacher asks one student to give the number names and the expanded form of the numbers just called out.

Conclusion: With the help of this activity, students can learn how to read and write numbers up to 200.

Concept Map

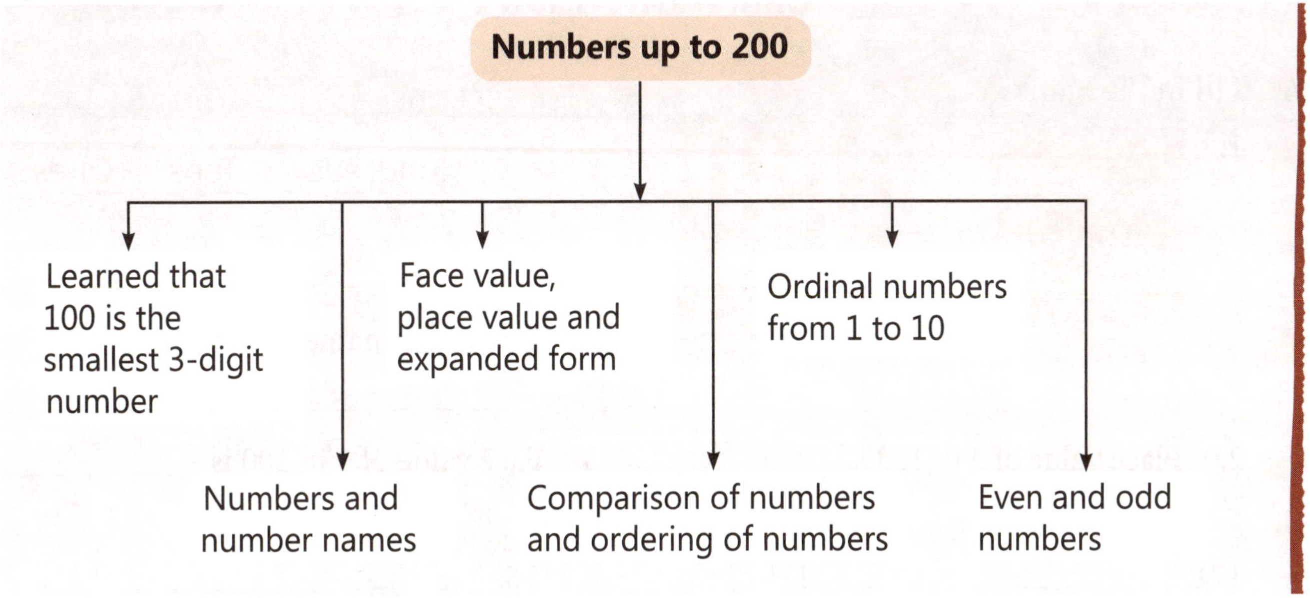

Key Concepts

- **One hundred:** The smallest 3-digit number, written as 100
- **Number name:** Representation of a number in words
- **Face value:** Face value of a digit is the digit itself.
- **Place value:** The value of each digit in a number
- **Expanded form:** The expanded form of a number is written as an addition statement of the place values of all the digits.
- **Comparing number:** To find out whether a number is greater than or less than or equal to another number
- **Ascending/Descending order:** Arranging numbers from smallest to greatest is ascending/increasing order and arranging numbers from greatest to smallest is descending/decreasing order.
- **Even and odd numbers:** Even numbers end with 2, 4, 6, 8 or 0 and odd numbers end with 1, 3, 5, 7 or 9.
- **Ordinal numbers:** It helps us to understand the position of objects like first, second, third and so on.

A. Fill in the blanks.

1. 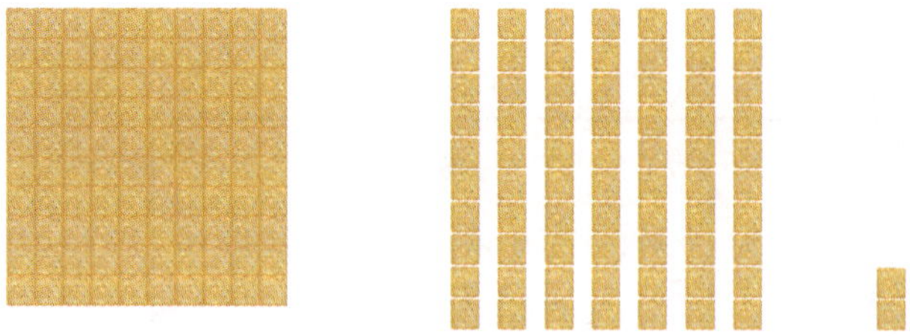

Hundreds	Tens	Ones

Number name = ____________

____

2. Place value of 5 in 153 is ____________.
3. Face value of 1 in 100 is ____________.

B. Complete the pattern.

171, __________, __________, 174, __________, 176, __________, __________.

C. Arrange the following numbers in ascending and descending order.

	Numbers	Ascending Order	Descending Order
1.	181, 175, 166, 109, 190		
2.	111, 101, 110, 114, 117		

D. Sid placed all his birthday gifts in a row.

Fill in the blanks.

1. Sid's favourite gift is placed second in the row. What is his favourite gift? __________
2. His best friend gave him the third gift. What did his best friend give him? __________
3. Sid loved the colour of the t-shirt. It is placed at the __________ position in the row.
4. Sid felt excited to show his __________ gift, that is, his new school bag to his friends.
5. His mother gave him the bicycle. Sid placed it at the __________ position in the row.

E. Place the even numbers in Bag A and odd numbers in Bag B.

200 49 5 136 140 18 192 165 100 62 178

SKILL UP!

A. 21 CS Critical Thinking

Collect buttons in 7 different colours.

Specify the colour of these buttons along with their ordinal numbers.

B. 21 CS Media Literacy IF

1 NO POVERTY

Find out the date of the 150th birth anniversary of Mahatma Gandhi in the year 2019. Prepare a birth anniversary chart based on your findings. Use number names and expanded forms of the numbers in your chart.

Also, find out a few famous sayings by Mahatma Gandhi and include in your chart. One of his famous sayings is given below.

"There's enough on this planet for everyone's need but not for everyone's greed."

C. 21 CS Information Literacy, Life Skills

Sarika's home address is given alongside.

Flat no. 3, 4th floor,
Tower 116, Tank Road

1. Which ordinal number is used in the address? ________
   Is it used for the flat number or for the floor number? ________
2. The flat number is less than the floor number. True or False. ________
3. Is the tower number an even number or an odd number? ________
4. How will you write the tower number in words? ________________

SUSTAINABLE DEVELOPMENT GOALS

Use Question B to start a discussion on the United Nations Sustainable Development Goals. The saying by Mahatma Gandhi, included in this question, can be linked to SDG 1 No Poverty. Many of his sayings can be linked to one or the other SDGs. Find out which of his sayings can be linked to which SDG.

Which SDG interests you the most? Choose an SDG and explore it more.

Worksheet 1

21 CS Critical Thinking HQ Happiness My Goal, Harmony In The Self

Fill in the blanks with the names of the children competing in the race.

1. __________ is coming first in the race.
2. __________ is coming second in the race.
3. __________ is coming fourth in the race.
4. __________ is coming fifth in the race.
5. __________ is coming last in the race.

Should the other children be happy for Farhan since he is coming first in the race? Yes/No

We should try our best but if we don't come first, it is all right. We must enjoy the sport!

2 Addition of 2-Digit Numbers

Learning Objectives

- To recall addition facts
- To add 1- and 2-digit numbers with 2-digit numbers (with and without regrouping)
- To add three 1-digit and three 2-digit numbers (with and without regrouping)
- To learn how to verify addition
- To solve word problems

Let's Get Started

21 CS Critical Thinking, Information Literacy   HQ Happiness My Goal

It is Annual Day in school. The participation of students of Class 2 in a few activities are listed below in the table.

Activity	Number of students participated
Singing	6
Dancing	5
Drawing	5
Swimming	7

What was the total number of students who participated?

____

WHAT IS ADDITION?

We add when we have to find the sum.

When we add, the value of something increases by the given amount.

The sign of addition is +, read as 'plus'.

> **NOTE**
>
> a. To add means to put things together.
>
> b. Addition is counting forward.

Addition Facts

1. When we add 1 to a number, we get the number just after it.

   $5 + 1 = 6$ $73 + 1 = 74$

2. When we add 0 to a number, the value of the number does not change.

   $43 + 0 = 43$ $99 + 0 = 99$

3. The sum of two numbers remains same when the order of numbers is changed.

   $2 + 3 = 5; 3 + 2 = 5$

   $5 + 4 = 9; 4 + 5 = 9$

MENTAL MATHS

1. 4 + 1 = ________
2. 93 + 0 = ________
3. 4 + 1 = 1 + ____ = ____

PUZZLE!

Match the spaceships with their creatures.

EXERCISE 2A

1. **Add the following.**

   a. 8 + 0 = ____ b. 54 + 1 = ____ c. 83 + 0 = ____ d. 36 + 1 = ____

2. **Add the following.**

   a. 0 + 5 = ____ b. 3 + 7 = 7 + ____ = ____ c. 4 + 3 = 3 + ____ = ____

ADDITION OF 1-DIGIT AND 2-DIGIT NUMBERS

This includes:

- Addition of 1-digit numbers with 2-digit numbers (with regrouping)
- Addition of two 2-digit numbers (with regrouping)
- Addition of three 1-digit numbers (with and without regrouping)
- Addition of three 2-digit numbers (with and without regrouping)

Addition of 1-Digit Numbers with 2-Digit Numbers with regrouping

We learnt addition of two 1-digit numbers and addition of 1-digit with 2-digit numbers without carrying forward in Class 1.

Let us see how we can add a 1-digit number with a 2-digit number with regrouping.

Example 1: Kanu bought 15 doughnuts. Meenu bought 8 doughnuts. Find the total number of doughnuts.

Solution: 15 is a 2-digit number and 8 is a 1-digit number. We must add 15 and 8 to find the total number of doughnuts.

Step 1: Add the digits in the ones place.

	T	O
	1	
	1	5
+		8
		3

15 has 1 ten and 5 ones.
8 has 8 ones.
Step 1: Add the ones.
So, 5 ones + 8 ones = 13 ones.
Write 3 of 13 in the ones place and carry over 1 of 13 to the tens place, as shown.

Step 2: Add the digits in tens place.

	T	O
	1	
	1	5
+		8
	2	3

Step 2: Add the tens.
The carried over 1 is added to the 1 of 15 to give 2 in the tens place.

The total number of doughnuts is **23**.

Common Errors

Always place the 1-digit number under the ones column.

	T	O
	3	5
+	3	

👎

	T	O
	3	5
+		3

👍

Always start the addition from the ones column.

	T	O
	1	
	4	6
+	2	4
	6	0

👎

	T	O
	1	
	4	6
+	2	4
	7	0

👍

Add all the digits in the tens column and then write the final sum.

	T	O
	3	5
+	1	5
	41	0

👎

	T	O
	1	
	3	5
+	1	5
	5	0

👍

Addition of Two 2-Digit Numbers with Regrouping

Radhika had two necklaces. The red necklace had 39 beads and the blue necklace had 15 beads. How many beads are there in all?

Since we have to find the number of beads in all, we must add them.

Step 1:

	T	O
	1	
	3	9
+	1	5
		4

In the ones column, 9 + 5 = 14. Now 14 is a 2-digit number, so we write '4' of 14 in the ones column and carry forward '1' of 14 and place it on top of 3 in the tens column.

Step 2:

	T	O
	1	
	3	9
+	1	5
	5	4

Now, add all the digits in the tens column, 1 + 3 + 1 = **5**.

Write 5 in the tens column.

There are 54 beads in all.

Exercise 2B

1. Regroup and add the following.

a.

	T	O
		6
+		5

b.

	T	O
	3	8
+	5	6

c.

	T	O
		7
+		4

d.

	T	O
	4	6
+	3	5

2. Find the sum.

a. 5 tens + 2 tens + 3 ones ______

b. 1 ten + 8 tens ______

c. 4 tens + 5 ones ______

d. 2 tens + 6 tens + 4 ones ______

Addition of Three 1-Digit Numbers

1. When we add three 1-digit numbers, we first add any two digits and then add the third digit to the sum of first two digits.

Example 2: Solve 2 + 3 + 4.

Solution: 2 + 3 + 4

First solve 2 + 3.

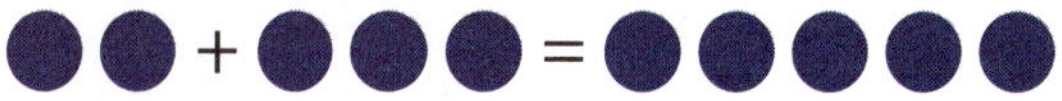

We get 5.

Now solve 5 + 4.

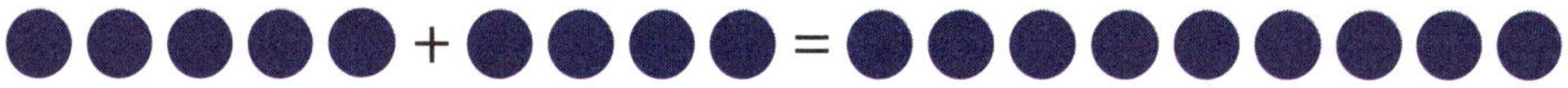

Thus, 5 + 4 = 9.

So, 2 + 3 + 4 = 9.

2. While adding three numbers, we should check if the sum of any two numbers is 10. If it is, then it becomes easier if we add the third number to 10 to get the answer.

Example 3: Solve 6 + 4 + 3.

6 + 4 + 3

10 + 3

6 + 4 = **10**

10 + 3 = **13**

6 + 4 + 3 = **13**

We can do this vertically too.

$$\begin{array}{r} 6 \\ 4 \\ +\ 3 \\ \hline \\ \hline \end{array} \quad (6 + 4 = 10) \qquad \begin{array}{r} 10 \\ +\ 3 \\ \hline \mathbf{13} \\ \hline \end{array}$$

Addition of three 2-digit numbers without regrouping

Rita bought 15 balloons, 23 party hats and 11 ice cream cones. How many items did she buy in all?

Number of balloons =

Number of party hats =

Number of ice cream cones =

	T	O
	1	5
	2	3
+	1	1
		9

In the ones column, 5 + 3 + 1 = **9**

Write 9 in the ones column.

	T	O
	1	5
	2	3
+	1	1
	4	9

In the tens column, 1 + 2 + 1 = 4

Write 4 in the tens column.

Thus, Rita bought 49 items in all.

NOTE

We know that

30 = 3 tens, 40 = 4 tens

So, we have

30 + 40 = 3 tens + 4 tens

	T	O
	3	0
+	4	0
	7	0

= 7 tens

More Examples:

1.

	T	O
	3	2
	1	4
+	2	3
	6	9

2.

	T	O
	1	0
	2	5
+	4	3
	7	8

This is the case of addition of three 2-digit numbers without carrying forward or without regrouping. Now, we will learn addition of three 2-digit numbers with regrouping.

Addition of three 2-digit numbers with regrouping

Example 4: In a parking area, there were 26 cars, 29 scooters and 38 motorcycles. How many vehicles were there in all?

Solution:

		T	O
Cars =		2	6
Scooters =		2	9
Motorcycles =	+	3	8
			3

In the ones column, 6 + 9 + 8 = **23.**

Write '3' of 23 in the ones column and carry forward '2' of 23 to the tens column.

	T	O
	2	
	2	6
	2	9
+	3	8
	9	3

Write '2' on top of 2 in the tens column.

In the tens column, 2 + 2 + 2 + 3 = **9.**

Write down 9 in the tens column.

Thus, there were 93 vehicles.

Do you know?

Plus is a Latin word which means 'more'. Latin is a language used in Italy. Robert Recorde, who designed the equals sign, introduced the plus sign to Britain in the year 1557.

Exercise 2C

1. Add the following.

a.

	O
	4
	1
+	3

b.

	O
	3
	2
+	4

c.

	T	O
		5
		5
+		7

d.

	T	O
		7
		3
+		6

2. Regroup and add the following.

a.

	T	O
	1	2
	3	4
+	2	3

b.

	T	O
	2	5
	3	0
+	4	2

c.

	T	O
	3	1
	2	4
+	1	3

d.

	T	O
	1	7
	4	3
+	3	6

VERIFYING ADDITION

We can check or verify addition by adding the numbers in the reverse order.

Examples:

1. Adding 39 and 22 will give the same result as adding 22 and 39.

	T	O
	1	
	3	9
+	2	2
	6	**1**

	T	O
	1	
	2	2
+	3	9
	6	**1**

2. Adding 12, 18 and 35 will give the same result as adding 35, 18 and 12.

	T	O
	1	
	1	2
	1	8
+	3	5
	6	**5**

	T	O
	1	
	3	5
	1	8
+	1	2
	6	**5**

EXERCISE 2D

Add and verify the solutions.

a.

	T	O
	3	4
+	4	8

Verify

	T	O

b.

	T	O
	1	4
+	2	6

Verify

	T	O

c.

	T	O
	7	4
+	1	9

Verify

	T	O

d.

	T	O
	3	5
	4	5
+	1	5

Verify

	T	O

GO EASY!

1. When we add the digits in the tens column (in case of carry forward to ten), the carried forward number must also be added with the tens digits.
2. Always start addition from the ones column.

WORD PROBLEMS

We add when we need to find the sum or total.

Example 5: 25 boys and 36 girls went to the park to play. How many children were there in all?

Solution:

		T	O
		1	
Boys =		2	5
Girls =	+	3	6
		6	**1**

Altogether, there were 61 children in the park.

NOTE

Look out for addition words in a problem.
Addition words:
Add, total, sum, plus, in all, altogether, more, increase, etc.

Example 6: Radhika bought 66 sweets, 15 chocolates and 18 ice creams for her party. How many items did she buy in all?

	T	O
	1	
	6	6
	1	5
+	1	8
	9	**9**

Radhika bought 99 items in all.

EXERCISE 2E

1. The teacher distributed 25 English books and 41 Maths books to the children in the class. How many books did she distribute in all?

2. For Rajan's birthday party, his mother bought 58 samosas and 35 pizzas. What is the total number of samosas and pizzas that she bought?
3. Ritika read 46 pages of her book on Saturday and 38 pages of her book on Sunday. How many pages did she read on both these days?
4. A shopkeeper sold 48 blue pens, 10 black pens and 27 red pens in one day. What is the total number of pens he sold that day?

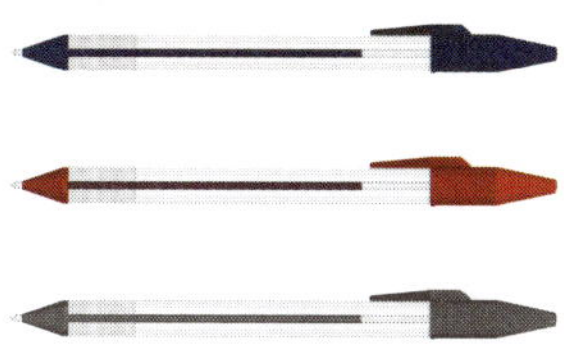

5. For the class picnic, the teacher bought 13 bottles of cola, 24 bottles of orange juice and 31 bottles of lemon juice. What was the total number of bottles that the teacher bought?

Mental Maths

1. 69 + ☐ = 70
2. 72 + 8 = ☐
3. 10 + 20 + 30 = ☐
4. 23 + 13 = 13 + ☐
5. The ones digit in the sum of 33 and 61 is ☐
6. 43 increased by 5 gives ☐
7. The next terms in the series 11, 22, 33, 44, ☐, ☐.
8. 4 tens + 5 tens + 3 ones = ☐

PUZZLE!

Guess the number of children!

1. At 8 o'clock in the morning, 30 children of Class 2 came to school.
2. At 9 o'clock, 12 more children of Class 2 entered the school.
3. By 10 o'clock, 71 more children entered the school premises, out of which 5 students belonged to Class 2.

What is the total number of students in Class 2? __________

CROSSWORD

Study the clues given alongside and fill in the crossword.

Across
1. 62 + 33
3. 69 + 5
4. 25 + 63
7. 38 + 15
10. 32 + 32
11. 70 + 10

Down
1. 43 + 47
2. 23 + 34
5. 56 + 31
6. 39 + 6
8. 62 + 23
9. 25 + 71
11. 56 + 24

Maths Lab Activity

21 CS Critical Thinking, Creativity and Innovation EL

Aim: To reinforce the addition of 1-digit and 2-digit numbers with the help of currency notes

Materials required: Currency notes of 10, 20 and 50 and coins of ₹1, ₹2 and ₹5

Procedure:

1. Collect the following currency notes.

4 fifty-rupee notes	10 twenty-rupee notes	20 ten-rupee notes

2. In how many ways can you make ₹50? One way is shown below. Think of two more ways for getting the sum as 50 using notes and coins of different denominations.

 +  +  = ₹50

How will you make ₹95 with the help of 10-rupee notes and one-rupee coins?

Concept Map

Addition of 2-digit numbers

- Addition facts
- Addition of 1-digit and 2-digit numbers with regrouping
- Addition of 2-digit numbers with and without regrouping
- Addition of three 1-digit numbers
- Addition of three 2-digit numbers with and without regrouping
- Verify addition
- Word problems
  - sum
  - in all
  - total
  - altogether

Key Concepts

- **Addition:** The process of finding the sum of numbers. Sum is another word used for addition, which shows the result obtained after adding two numbers.
- **Carrying forward:** While carrying forward, we keep one part of the sum in the ones column and carry the other part to the tens column, to add it with the numbers in the tens column. This concept is known as **regrouping**.
- **Addition facts:**
  - When we add 0 to a number, the value of the number does not change.
  - When we add 1 to a number, we get the number just after it.
  - The sum of two numbers remains the same when the order of numbers is changed.
- We learnt addition of 1- and 2-digit numbers with 2-digit numbers with regrouping, addition of three 1-digit and three 2-digit numbers with regrouping.
- While verifying an addition problem, the numbers must be added in the reverse order again.
- **Word problems on addition:** Questions of addition based on our daily lives

A. Choose the correct option.

1. 18 + 22 is same as

   a. Forty-one b. Forty c. Forty-two d. Forty-three

2. Which two digits can be combined for easier addition in 4 + 2 + 6?

   a. 4 and 2 b. 4 and 6 c. 2 and 6

3. 22 + 33 + 27 gives digit ____________ in the tens place.

   a. 9 b. 7 c. 8 d. 6

B. Match the following.

Column A	Column B
1. 50 + 30	48 + 10 + 37
2. 20 + 21 + 35	17
3. 7 + 8 + 2	Thirty
4. Ninety-five	35 + 21 + 20
5. 1 + 29	8 tens

C. Regroup and add.

1.

	T	O
	5	9
+		5

2.

	T	O
		6
		6
+		6

3.

	T	O
	3	7
	3	7
+	1	0

4.

	T	O
	4	9
+	1	7

D. Fill in the blanks.

1. 33 + 37 = ________
2. 4 tens + 3 tens = ________
3. The sum of 23 and 37 is ________
4. ________ is added to a number to get the next number.

E. Write T for true and F for false.

1. The number name for the sum of 20 and 36 is fifty-six. ☐
2. 15 + 0 + 1 = 15 ☐
3. When zero is added to a number, the answer is one more than the given number. ☐

F. Answer the following.

1. What is the sum of the smallest 2-digit number and greatest 1-digit number?
2. Karuna scored 30 marks, Sheena scored 35 marks and Tina scored 29 marks in a Mathematics test. What is the total marks scored by all of them?

SKILL UP!

A. 21 CS Critical Thinking

Find out the total number of students in any two sections of Class 2 in your school. Add the counts and find the total number of students.

B. 21 CS Critical Thinking, Information Literacy CC Integration with English

Look at the sentence given below.

'I love my Mathematics book very much'.

Write the number of vowels = ______

Write the number of consonants = ______

Add the vowels and the consonants.

	T	O
+		

C. 21 CS Life Skills HQ Happiness My Goal

3 GOOD HEALTH AND WELL-BEING

Sumit, Nungsang and Raheem went to the park in the evening. Sumit ran 24 rounds of the park, Nungsang ran 20 rounds and Raheem ran 32 rounds. The children felt very good after the exercise and decided to do it every day.

What was the total number of rounds that all the three children took? Is it good to exercise everyday?

SUSTAINABLE DEVELOPMENT GOALS

Question C is in line with SDG 3 Good Health and Well-Being. What is the importance of good health? What kind of actions can you take to achieve SDG 3?

Worksheet 2

21 CS Critical Thinking, Information Literacy — STEAM CHALLENGE

Anu and Hazel went to a balloon seller. The balloon seller had numbered his balloons from 1 to 30. Each kid selected two sets of three balloons using the conditions given below.

a. Number on one balloon is the sum of the other two.

b. The sum is in between 20 and 30

c. The sum can be equal to 20 or 30.

Fill the blank spaces inside the balloons with the numbers selected by Anu and Hazel based on the conditions given.

(*Hint:* Observe the colour of the blank balloons. Identify the numbers corresponding to the colours from the list of balloons with numbers.)

3 Subtraction of 2-Digit Numbers

Learning Objectives

- To understand that subtraction means to "take away"
- To recall subtraction facts
- To subtract 1- and 2-digit numbers from 2-digit numbers with regrouping
- To verify subtraction using addition
- To solve word problems on subtraction

Let's Get Started

21 CS Critical Thinking, Life Skills EL

A boy saw 13 birds in his garden. His mother asked him how many birds would be left if any 2 birds fly away?

There are 13 birds.

Cross out 2 birds.

We can count the number of birds left on our fingers as well.

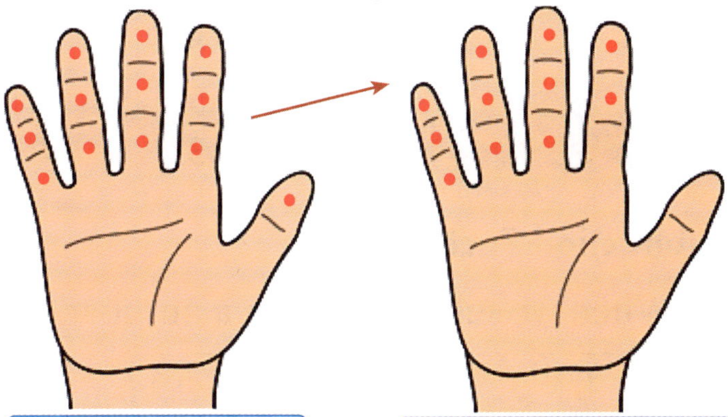

Count 13 dots on your fingers.

Remove 2 dots from your fingers.

Count what you are left with. You will be left with 11.
So, 11 birds will be left.

	T	O
	1	3
−		2
	1	**1**

WHAT IS SUBTRACTION?

We subtract when

- we have to take away some quantity from another quantity or
- the value of something is going to decrease by a given amount

The sign of subtraction is –, read as 'minus'.

NOTE

In subtraction, the bigger number is always written on the top. That is, we always subtract the smaller number from the bigger number.

	T	O
	5	6
–	8	9

(wrong)

	T	O
	8	9
–	5	6

(right)

Terms Used in Subtraction

- **Subtrahend** is the number to be subtracted.
- **Minuend** is the greater number from which the smaller number (subtrahend) is subtracted.
- **Difference** is another word used for subtraction, which means the result obtained after subtracting two numbers.

Example 1: Solve 28 – 5.

	T	O
	2	8
–		5
	2	**3**

We have,
28 – 5 = **23**
28 is the minuend.
5 is the subtrahend.
23 is the difference between 28 and 5.

Subtraction Facts

1. When we subtract 0 from a number, the value of the number does not change.

   5 – 0 = **5**   49 – 0 = **49**   98 – 0 = **98**

2. When we subtract the number from itself, we get zero.

   17 – 17 = **0**   56 – 56 = **0**   83 – 83 = **0**

3. When we subtract 1 from a number, we get the number just before it.

   29 – 1 = **28**   37 – 1 = **36**   85 – 1 = **84**

MENTAL MATHS

1. 72 – 0 = ____________
2. 76 – 76 = ____________
3. 18 – 1 = ____________

SUBTRACTION WITH REGROUPING

Let us learn how to perform subtraction of

- 1-digit numbers from 2-digit numbers
- 2-digit numbers from 2-digit numbers

Subtraction of 1-Digit Numbers from 2-Digit Numbers with Regrouping

Rohit has 23 candies. Sara asked him to give her 8 candies. How many candies will be left with Rohit?

Here, we need to subtract 8 from 23, that is, 23 – 8. We write

	T	O
	2	3
–		8

First, subtract 8 from 3 in the ones column. But, 8 is bigger than 3, so we cannot subtract.

	T	O
	1	13
	~~2~~	~~3~~
–		8

In this case, borrow 1 from 2 in the tens column. Then, 3 in the ones column becomes 13 and 2 in the tens column becomes 1 (since 2 – 1 = **1**). We write 13 above 8.

	T	O
	1	13
	~~2~~	~~3~~
–		8
	1	**5**

In the ones column, 13 – 8 = **5** and in the tens column, we are left with 1. So, 23 – 8 = **15**.

Subtraction of 2-Digit Numbers from 2-Digit Numbers with Regrouping

Ajay had total 25 red and green marbles. Out of them, 18 marbles were red. How many marbles were green?

Cross out 18 red marbles. We get 7 green marbles. Now, let us solve this as a subtraction problem.

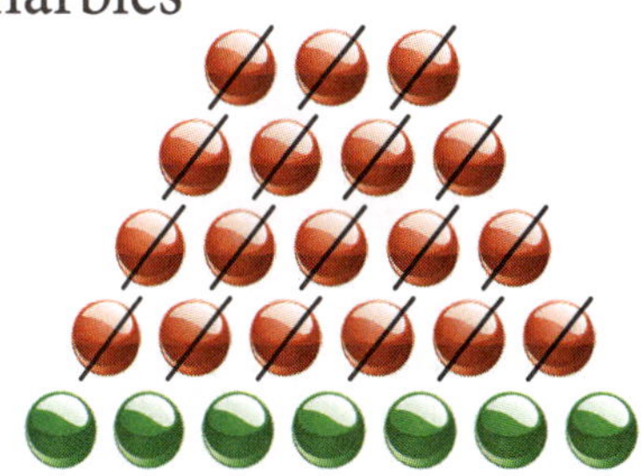

		T	O
Total number of marbles =		2	5
Red marbles =	–	1	8

In the ones column, 8 is greater than 5, so we cannot subtract 8 from 5. We borrow 1 from '2' in the tens column.

	T	O
	1	15
	2	5
−	1	8
		7

'2' in the tens column becomes 1 and '5' in the ones column becomes 15.

Now 15 − 8 = 7

	T	O
	1	15
	2	5
−	1	8
	0	7

Write 7 in the ones column and in the tens column 1 − 1 = 0.
Hence, there are 7 green marbles.

COMMON ERRORS

	T	O
		10
	5	0
−		3
	5	7

	T	O
	4	10
	5	0
−		3
	4	7

Let us see the subtraction where the greater number has 0 at the ones place.

Consider 30 − 6.

	T	O
	2	10
	3	0
−		6
	2	4

In this case, borrow 1 ten from tens place and regroup 1 ten to 10 ones.

That is, cross out 0 in the ones place and write 10 over it. Also, cross out 3 in the tens place and write 2 over it.

Now, there are 2 tens and 10 ones in 30.

Take away 6 ones from 10 ones, to get 4 ones. In the tens place, we are left with only 2. Hence, we get 24 as the answer.

EXERCISE 3A

Solve the following.

1.

	T	O
	8	5
−		7

2.

	T	O
	6	4
−	2	9

3.

	T	O
	7	3
−		5

4.

	T	O
	9	0
−	5	6

5.

	T	O
	6	4
−		8

6.

	T	O
	3	5
−	1	7

7.

	T	O
	8	0
−	4	5

8.

	T	O
	7	1
−	3	6

VERIFYING SUBTRACTION USING ADDITION

A simple method to check or verify the result of subtraction using addition that works for regrouping problems as well is explained below.

A shopkeeper has 85 notebooks to sell. He sold 63 of them. Find the number of notebooks left with the shopkeeper.

We write this as

	T	O
Total number of notebooks =	8	5
Number of notebooks sold = −	6	3
Number of notebooks left =	**2**	**2**

He is left with 22 notebooks.

Verify

	T	O
	2	2
+	6	3
	8	**5**

The shopkeeper wishes to check if he has counted the leftover notebooks correctly.

How to verify?

The number of notebooks left (that is, the answer), if added to the number of notebooks sold should give him the total number of notebooks.

This means that the total quantity (85 here) in question should always match.

The answer must not be added to the total quantity in question. The total quantity in question must be the answer of the verification process.

EXERCISE 3B

Find the difference and verify the result using addition.

1.

	T	O
	5	4
−	2	3

Verify

	T	O
+		

2.

	T	O
	9	5
−	1	3

Verify

	T	O
+		

3.

	T	O
	6	5
−	2	3

Verify

	T	O
+		

WORD PROBLEMS

We subtract when we know that the answer is going to reduce by the number given.

NOTE

Look out for subtraction words in a problem. Words like:

Subtract, difference, minus, take away, deduct, decrease, less than, reduce by, how many were left, how many more, by how much, etc.

Examples:

1. 24 less than 56 is written as

	T	O
	5	6
–	2	4
	3	**2**

In the ones column, 6 – 4 = **2**
In the tens column, 5 – 2 = **3**

56 – 24 = **32**

2. Take away 47 from 93. This is written as

	T	O
	9	3
–	4	7

	T	O
	8	13
	~~9~~	~~3~~
–	4	7
	4	**6**

GO EASY!

The number written after the word 'from' is the bigger number and must be kept on top while subtracting.

93 – 47 = **46**

3. Monu weighs 56 kg. Sonu weighs 13 kg less than Monu. How much does Sonu weigh?

		T	O
Monu weighs		5	6
Sonu would weigh less by	–	1	3
		4	**3**

Therefore, Sonu weighs 43 kg.

4. Banrap bought 85 mango ice creams for some guests at home. 29 ice creams melted on his way. How many ice creams were still ready to be eaten?

	T	O
	7	15
Total number of ice creams =	~~8~~	~~5~~
Number of melted ice creams = −	2	9
	5	**6**

So, 56 ice creams were still ready to be eaten.

Exercise 3C

Solve the following and verify by using addition.

1. 38 less than 59 is

	T	O
	5	9
−	3	8

Verify

	T	O
+		

2. Take away 77 from 78

	T	O
	7	8
−	7	7

Verify

	T	O
+		

3. Out of 76 toffees, the teacher distributed 54 toffees, how many toffees were left?

4. There were 93 cars parked in the car parking area. 48 of them were blue cars and the rest were all red cars. How many red cars were there?

5. Out of 65 roses at the florist's shop, 54 roses were red. The rest of the roses were pink. How many roses were pink?

6. In a classroom, there were 56 chairs and 41 tables. How many more chairs were there than tables?

MENTAL MATHS

1. Out of the numbers given, choose different pairs of numbers whose difference is 10.

   10 29 55 52 62 39 45 20

2. Take out 4 tens from 80 ____________.
3. 87 is 1 less than ____________.
4. a. 10 subtracted from 90 gives ____________.

   b. 50 subtracted from the above result gives ____________.

PUZZLE!

The teacher of Class 2 announced the marks obtained by students in a Maths test in the form of a puzzle.

She said that,

1. Anil got 95 – 12 = ___________ marks in the test.
2. Sumit got 18 marks less than 98 = ___________ marks in the test.
3. Sid got 10 marks less than Anil's marks. He got ___________ marks.
4. If you take away 8 from 83, you will get the marks that Ameeta got. She got ___________ marks.
5. Sana got 15 marks less than Ameeta. She got ___________ marks.

Do you know?

The method of subtraction, that is, **borrowing**, originated somewhere around the year 1200. The word borrow, was not commonly used until around the year 1600. It was discovered when there was a situation to take 6 out of nothing, that is zero.

Maths Lab Activity

21 CS Critical Thinking, Collaboration | EL | HQ Happiness My Goal

Aim: To understand the concept of subtraction of two 2-digit numbers

Materials required: Playing cards, a notebook, a pencil

Procedure:

1. Divide the whole class into two teams. Let each team have a set of playing cards. Take out all Jacks, Queens and the Kings. Let each team take out 2 cards to make two 2-digit numbers.
2. Both the teams should now find out the difference between these two 2-digit numbers. The team that finds the result faster wins.

1 6 8 2

	T	O
	7	12
	~~8~~	~~2~~
–	1	6
	6	6

Since 82 is bigger, we subtract 16 from 82.

82 – 16 = **66**

Conclusion: This will help students to learn subtraction of two 2-digit numbers with regrouping faster.

Concept Map

Subtraction of 2-digit numbers

- Subtraction facts
- To subtract 1- and 2-digit numbers from 2-digit numbers with regrouping
- Verifying subtraction using addition
- Word problems
  - minus
  - take away
  - by how much
  - difference
  - subtract
  - decrease
  - less than

Key Concepts

- **Subtraction:** The process of taking away one number from another number. If the value of a quantity or a number decreases, we subtract.
- **Difference:** Another word used for subtraction, which means the **result** obtained after subtracting two numbers.
- **Subtraction words:** Subtract, difference, minus, take away, deduct, decrease, less than, reduce by, how many were left, how many more, by how much, etc.
- **Regrouping in subtraction:** When we cannot subtract a bigger number from a smaller number at ones place, we borrow 1 ten and add it to the number in the ones value. 1 ten = 10 ones. This concept is called **regrouping** in subtraction.
- **Subtrahend:** The number to be subtracted
- **Minuend:** The greater number from which the smaller number (subtrahend) is subtracted
- **Subtraction facts:**
  - When we subtract 0 from a number, the value of the number does not change.
  - When we subtract the number from itself, we get zero.
  - When we subtract 1 from a number, we get the number just before it.
- We learnt, subtraction of 1- and 2-digit numbers with regrouping.
- While verifying a subtraction problem, the total quantity in question must be the answer of the verification process.

A. Solve the following.

1.

	T	O
	4	7
−	1	1

2.

	T	O
	6	9
−	2	8

3.

	T	O
	6	5
−	1	5

4.

	T	O
	3	4
−	2	0

B. Subtract the following.

	T	O
	7	4
−	2	9

Circle all the numbers that are greater than the answer.

174 62 9

12 31 6 180

89 158 44

C. Match the following.

Column A **Column B**

1.

	T	O
	7	4
−	2	0

13

2.

	T	O
	3	8
−	2	5

36

3.

	T	O
	9	2
−	5	6

42

4.

	T	O
	8	9
−	4	7

54

D. Subtract and verify.

1.

	T	O
	5	4
−	2	3

Verify

	T	O
+		

2.

	T	O
	9	5
−	1	3

Verify

	T	O
+		

E. Write T for true and F for false.

1. We subtract the bigger number from the smaller number always. ☐
2. If we subtract a number from itself, we get 1. ☐
3. 10 less than 90 is 100. ☐
4. 23 taken away from 55 is 32. ☐

F. Fill in the blanks.

1. There are 98 – 10 = ________________ children in Class 2.
2. Sachin wanted to give each child a chocolate.

   He brought 84 – 12 = ________________ chocolates.

3. He needs ________________ more chocolates.

G. Solve the following word problems.

1. Sarobara bought 99 balloons.
   a. She put up 51 balloons for her birthday party. How many balloons was she left with?
   b. She hung 6 balloons around her birthday cake. How many balloons was she left with then?

2. Out of 75 monkeys in a zoo, 22 ran away. How many monkeys were left in the zoo?

3. Out of 76 children in a class, 52 children came by car. The rest of the children came in the school bus. How many children came in the school bus?

SKILL UP!

A. 21 CS Collaboration | EL

Make two teams. Give each team two dice to roll. When each team rolls the dice, we get a 2-digit number. Tell them to form two 2-digit numbers alternatively each time and then find the difference between them.

B. 21 CS Critical Thinking, Life Skills | CC Integration with Physical Education | HQ Cooperation and Collaborative Living

3 GOOD HEALTH AND WELL-BEING

34 children were running in a race. Out of them, Ameer fell and hurt himself. Two other participants, Sumit and Rajdeep, stopped and helped Ameer get up and took him to the side of the racing track.

How many children could complete the race? ____________

Have you ever participated in a racing competition? ____________

Have you ever helped someone in need? Which is more important, winning or participating? ____________________________________

C. 21 CS Critical Thinking, Information Literacy | CC Integration with English

Read the proverb.

'The grass is always greener on the other side of the fence'.

Write down all the vowels and the consonants. Count them and find the difference between the number of consonants and the number of vowels.

(*Hint:* There are 26 letters in the English alphabet. The letters a, e, i, o and u are called vowels. The other letters are called consonants.)

SUSTAINABLE DEVELOPMENT GOALS

Question B is in line with SDG 3 Good Health and Well-Being. What is the importance of good health and well-being? Do you know that doing exercise while playing sports is one of the best ways to stay healthy?

WORKSHEET 3

21 CS Critical Thinking AI

Solve the subtraction problems. Use the colour codes to colour the picture.

(*Hint:* The background of the picture is light green in colour.)

Colour Codes

56 = Light green 42 = Yellow

68 = Orange 66 = Blue

a. 88 − 20 = ____

b. 90 − 48 = ____

c. 90 − 22 = ____

d. 92 − 50 = ____

e. 99 − 31 = ____

f. 82 − 40 = ____

g. 89 − 21 = ____

h. 89 − 47 = ____

i. 79 − 11 = ____

j. 71 − 29 = ____

k. 88 − 20 = ____

l. 80 − 38 = ____

m. 90 − 24 = ____

n. 79 − 23 = ____

o. 92 − 36 = ____

p. 98 − 42 = ____

q. 80 − 24 = ____

4 Numbers up to 1000

Learning Objectives

- To learn about 3-digit numbers and represent them on the number line
- To understand place value, face value and expanded form of 3-digit numbers
- To compare and order 3-digit numbers
- To find numbers before, after and in-between the other numbers
- To form numbers from the given digits

Let's Get Started

21 CS Critical Thinking, Information Literacy

Given below are pictures of Ameeta's family members with their ages.

Ameeta's Grandmother

89 years

Ameeta's Father

61 years

Ameeta's Mother

54 years

Ameeta

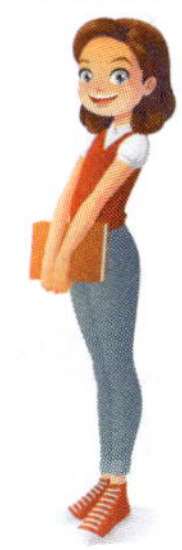

24 years

1. Write the number name of Ameeta's:
   a. Father's age _______________ b. Mother's age _______________
2. Find Ameeta's grandfather's age, if he is three years older than Ameeta's grandmother.
   a. (in numerals) ____________ b. (in words) ____________
3. Write Ameeta's friend's age, if she is one year younger than Ameeta. (in words) ____
4. Arrange the age of each member in ascending order.
   ____

5. Fill in the blanks.
   a. 89 = ______ tens ______ ones b. 92 = ______ tens ______ ones
   c. In 61, place value of 6 is ______ and face value of 6 is ______.

INTRODUCTION TO 3-DIGIT NUMBERS

Rohit has 99 colourful marbles. He bought one more marble. How many marbles does he have now?

Adding 1 marble to 99 marbles, we get,

	H	T	O
		9	9
+			1
	1	0	0

Hundreds	Tens	Ones
1	0	0

Do you know?

A 100 years make a century.

When you score 100 runs in cricket match, it is also known as a century.

It introduces the place value of **hundreds** after ones and tens.

The **number name** for 100 is **one hundred**.

100 can be represented by the block shown below.

Note

100 is the smallest 3-digit number.

This block has one hundred squares. There are 10 squares in each row and in each column.

	Numeral	Number Name
	100	One hundred
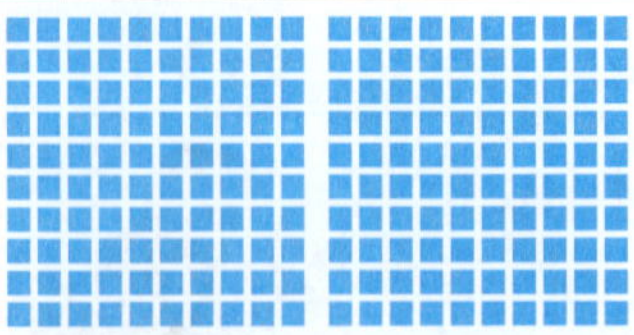	200	Two hundred
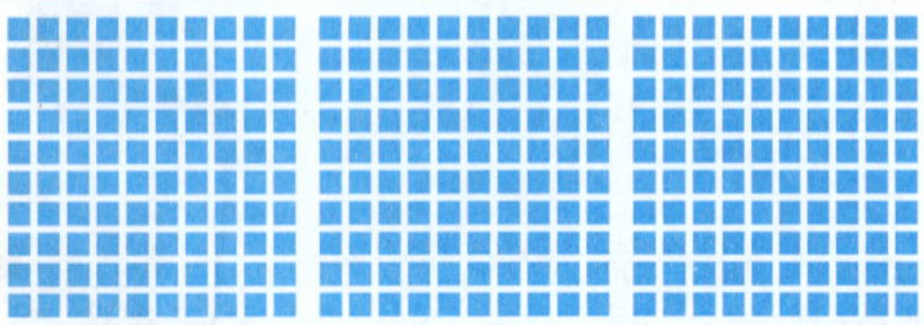	300	Three hundred
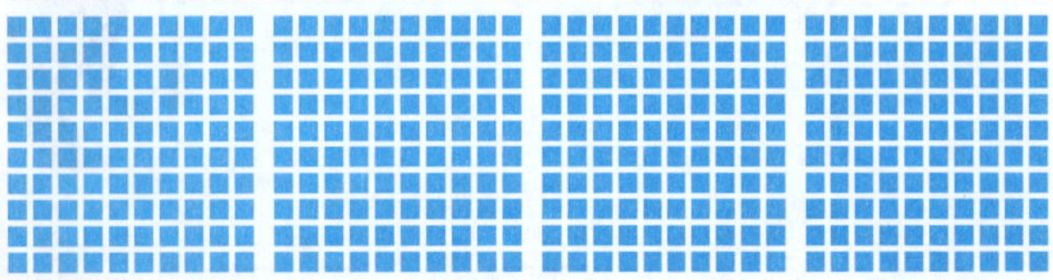	400	Four hundred

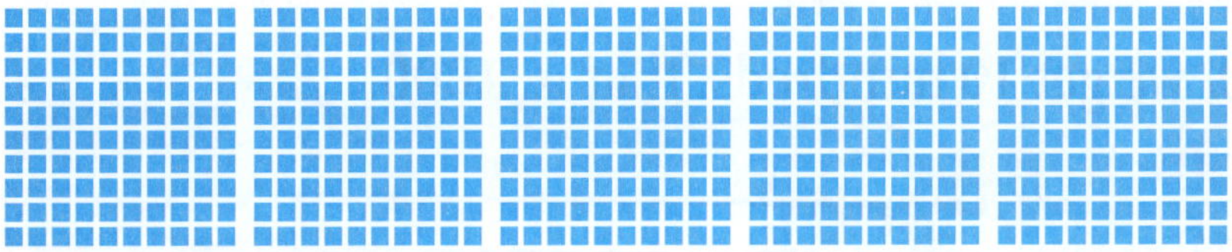	500	Five hundred
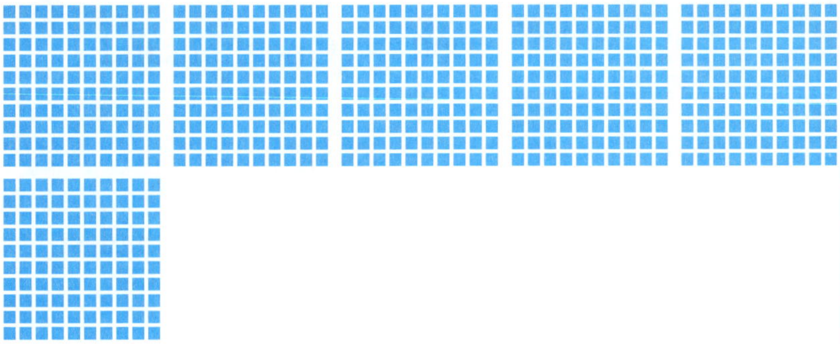	600	Six hundred
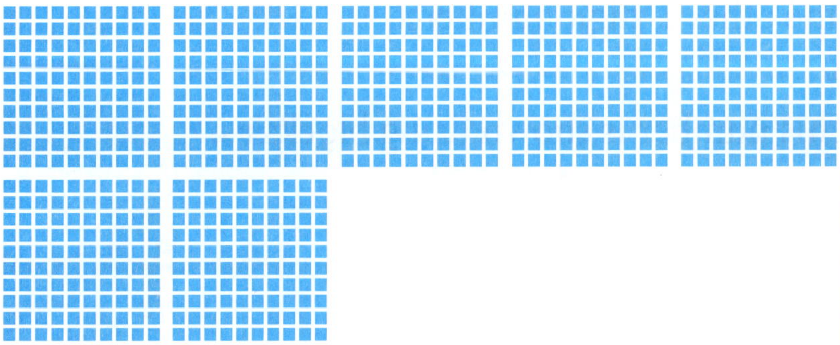	700	Seven hundred
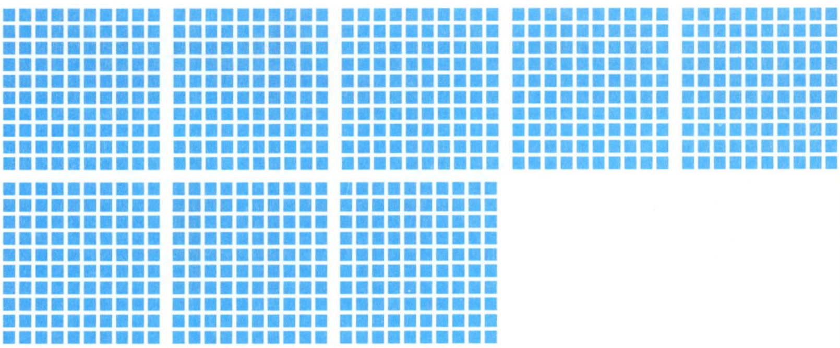	800	Eight hundred
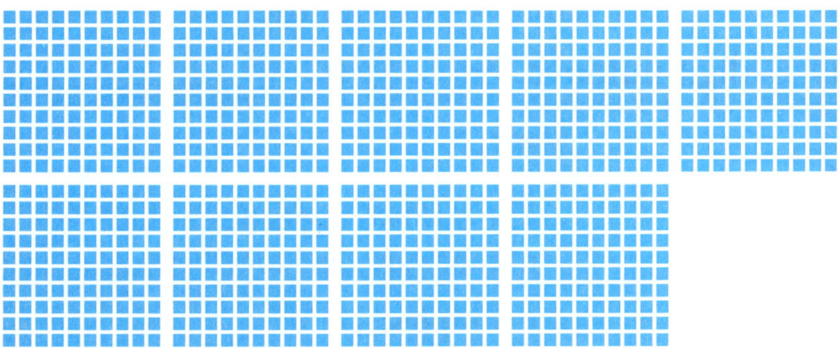	900	Nine hundred

The Number 1000

By combining ten blocks of 100, we get 10 hundreds, that is, **1000**.

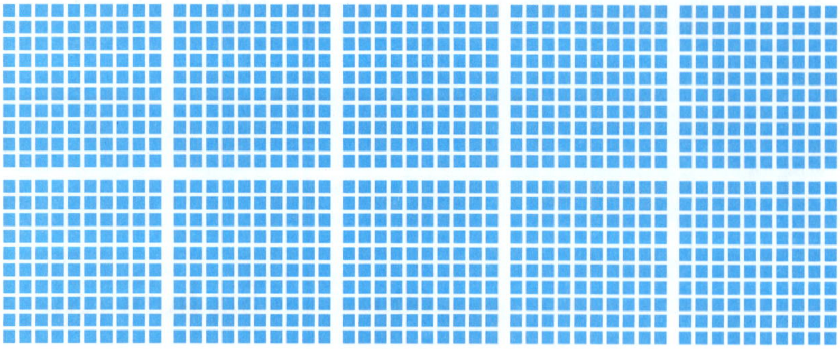

1000 One thousand

1000 is read as **one thousand**.

> **NOTE**
> 1000 is the smallest 4-digit number.

More 3-digit Numbers

Let us learn and understand some other 3-digit numbers.

Consider a 3-digit number, 104.

We can represent it as

Hundreds	Tens	Ones
1	0	4

This number is shown using blocks as:

1 hundred 4 ones

Number name = One hundred four

Consider the number 247.

Hundreds	Tens	Ones
2	4	7

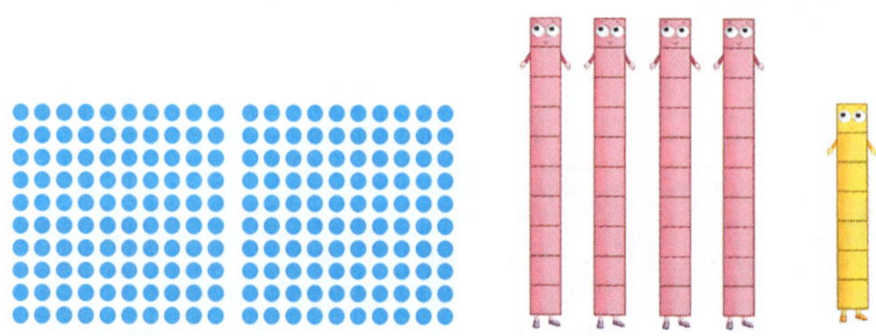

2 hundreds 4 tens 7 ones

Number name = Two hundred forty-seven

Let us now have a look at another 3-digit number, 593.

How do we read 593?

593 is read as five hundred ninety-three.

H	T	O
5	9	3
↓	↓	↓
Five hundred	ninety	three

> **NOTE**
> The last two digits of a 3-digit number are read together.
>
> **Examples:**
>
> 4<u>72</u> = Four hundred <u>seventy-two</u>
>
> 3<u>99</u> = Three hundred <u>ninety-nine</u>

EXERCISE 4A

1. Fill in the blanks.

a. 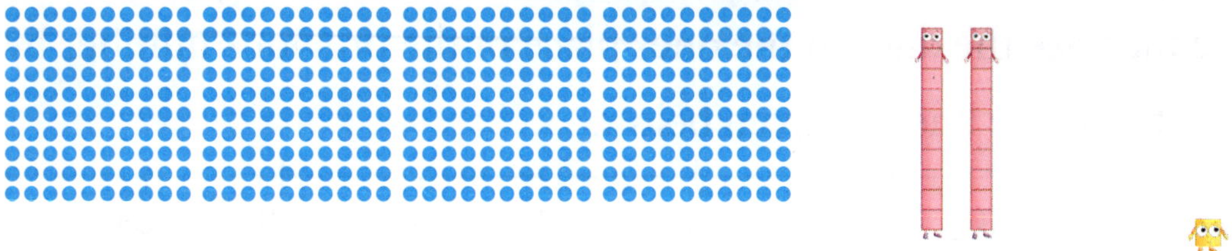

____ hundreds ____ tens ____ ones

Number name = ______________________________

b. 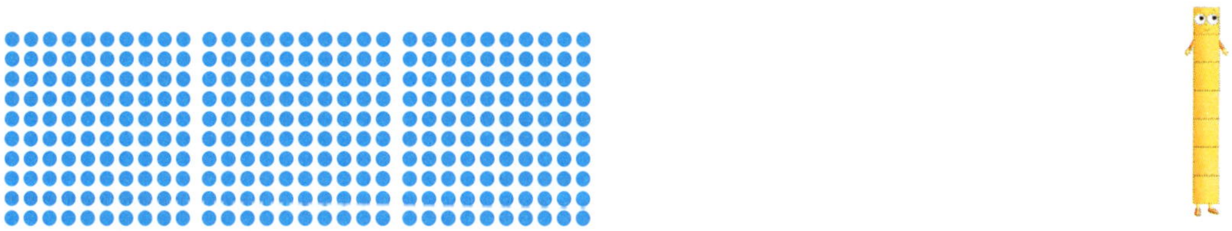

____ hundreds ____ ones

Number name = ______________________________

c. 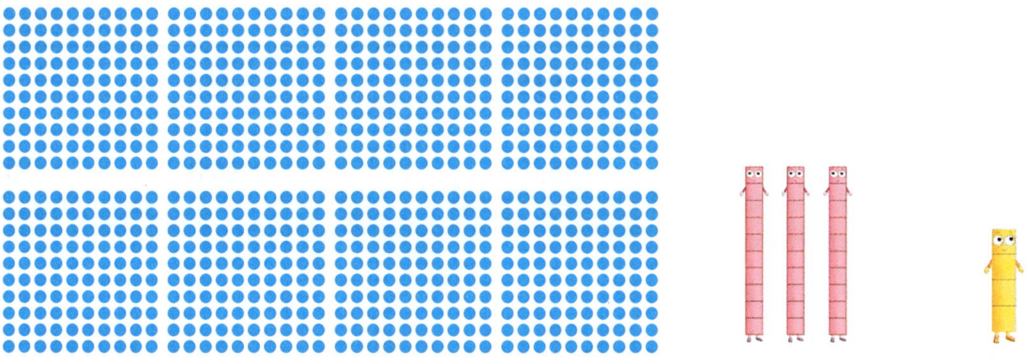

____ hundreds ____ tens ____ ones

Number name = ______________________________

2. Fill in the blanks.

a. 906 = ________ hundreds ________ tens ________ ones

Number name = ______________________________

b. 243 = ________ hundreds ________ tens ________ ones

Number name = ______________________________

3. Write the numerals.

a. Four hundred thirty-one ________

b. Nine hundred sixty-three ________

c. Six hundred nineteen ________

d. Eight hundred seventy-one ________

REPRESENTATION OF 3-DIGIT NUMBERS ON NUMBER LINE

The number line is a line which shows the order of numbers as we count them. The number line can be extended by adding 1 every time. To get to the next number, we increase the digit in the ones place of the previous number by 1.

Some parts of number line are given below.

101 102 103 104 105 106 107 108 109 110

511 512 513 514 515 516 517 518 519 520

EXERCISE 4B

Fill in the missing numbers on the number lines.

1. 321 322 ... 325 ... 329 330
2. 541 ... 544 ... 547 ... 550
3. 831 ... 835 ... 838 ...
4. 671 ... 675 ... 678 ... 680

PLACE VALUE AND FACE VALUE

Place Value: In numbers, each digit is assigned a value. It is referred to as its place value.

Let us learn about the place value of 3-digit numbers.

NOTE

To write the place value of a number, write the number followed by as many zeros, as there are digits to the right of the number.

Examples: Consider the following numbers.

1. 539

H	T	O
5	3	9

The place value of 5 is 500.
The place value of 3 is 30.
The place value of 9 is 9.

2. 721

H	T	O
7	2	1

The place value of 7 is 700.
The place value of 2 is 20.
The place value of 1 is 1.

Face Value: The face value of a digit is the digit itself.

Examples: Consider the numbers, 539 and 721.

H	T	O
5	3	9

The face value of 5 is 5.
The face value of 3 is 3.
The face value of 9 is 9.

H	T	O
7	2	1

The face value of 7 is 7.
The face value of 2 is 2.
The face value of 1 is 1.

EXPANDED FORM OF 3-DIGIT NUMBERS

Consider the following examples to learn expanded form of 3-digit numbers.

Example 1: Write the expanded form of 258.

H	T	O
2	5	8

= 2 hundreds + 5 tens + 8 ones
or 258 = 200 + 50 + 8

Example 2: Write the expanded form of 973.

H	T	O
9	7	3

= 9 hundreds + 7 tens + 3 ones
or 973 = 900 + 70 + 3

NOTE

If the expanded form of a number is 200 + 90 + 9, then its short form is 299.

Example: Short form of 800 + 70 + 3 is 873.

COMMON ERRORS

Expanded form of 349

349 = 3 + 4 + 9 ✗

349 = 300 + 40 + 9 ✓

EXERCISE 4C

1. Write the place values and the face values.

a. 173

Place value of	Face value of
1 = ________	1 = ________
7 = ________	7 = ________
3 = ________	3 = ________

b. 684

Place value of	Face value of
6 = ________	6 = ________
8 = ________	8 = ________
4 = ________	4 = ________

2. Write in expanded form.

a. 385 = ____________ hundreds ____________ tens ____________ ones

OR

385 = ____________ + ____________ + ____________

b. 691 = ____________ hundreds ____________ tens ____________ one

OR

691 = ____________ + ____________ + ____________

3. **Write the place value of the underlined digits.**

a. $\underline{3}81$ ____ b. $4\underline{7}6$ ____ c. $59\underline{2}$ ____

4. **Write the face value of the underlined digits.**

a. $1\underline{4}8$ ____ b. $\underline{9}37$ ____ c. $25\underline{6}$ ____

5. **Fill in the blanks.**

a. Short form of 500 + 30 + 2 = ____________

b. Face value of 7 in 107 = ____________

c. Place value of 4 in 849 = ____________

d. Expanded form of 909 = ____________

COMPARING NUMBERS

Let us compare and find:

- greater or lesser of the two numbers
- greatest or smallest among more than two numbers

NOTE

Out of the two numbers being compared, the number with more number of digits is always the greater number.

- **When the number of digits is different.**

Which number is greater?

T	O
6	3

OR

H	T	O
1	5	8

63 is a 2-digit number. 158 is a 3-digit number.

$158 > 63$

- **When the number of digits is same.**

a.

H	T	O
$\underline{4}$	6	7

OR

H	T	O
$\underline{9}$	3	5

Check the digits placed at the hundreds place in both the numbers and compare.

We know that 9 is greater than 4. Therefore, $467 < 935$.

COMMON ERRORS

$99 > 300$ (wrong) $99 < 300$ (right)

99 starts with a 9 and 300 starts with a 3.

But 300 is bigger, because it is a 3-digit number.

99 is a 2-digit number.

b.

H	T	O
6	7	3

OR

H	T	O
6	2	4

The digits placed at the hundreds place are same, that is, 6.

Now, check the digits placed at the tens place in both the numbers and compare.

7 is greater than 2. Therefore, 673 [>] 624.

c.

H	T	O
1	2	5

OR

H	T	O
1	2	6

H	T	O
1	2	5

H	T	O
1	2	6

Here we find that the digits at the hundreds place in both the numbers are 1.

H	T	O
1	2	5

H	T	O
1	2	6

Here we find that the digits at the tens place in both the numbers are 2.

H	T	O
1	2	5

H	T	O
1	2	6

The digits at the ones place in both the numbers are 5 and 6. 6 is greater than 5. Therefore, 125 [<] 126.

- **When all the three digits are same and placed in the same way, then both the numbers are equal.**

H	T	O
9	6	7

OR

H	T	O
9	6	7

The digits at the hundreds place, tens place and ones place in both the numbers are same. They are 9, 6 and 7, respectively.

Therefore, 967 [=] 967.

Exercise 4D

1. Compare the numbers and put the correct sign (>, < or =).

a. 964 [ ] 182 b. 729 [ ] 607 c. 200 [ ] 800

d. 521 [ ] 906 e. 374 [ ] 374 f. 189 [ ] 183

2. Encircle the greatest number in each set of numbers.

a. 237, 569, 481 b. 729, 843, 669 c. 485, 127, 489

3. Encircle the smallest number in each set of numbers.

a. 478, 926, 650 b. 769, 238, 815 c. 347, 529, 341

ORDERING OF NUMBERS

Ascending order of numbers means **numbers written in an increasing order.**

Example: 156, 204, 739, 845

Ascending order means arranging from smallest to greatest.

Descending order of numbers means **numbers written in a decreasing order.**

Example: 973, 805, 612, 497

Descending order means arranging from greatest to smallest.

Example 3: Arrange the numbers in ascending order.

629, 173, 805, 467

Solution:

Step 1: Check the digits placed at the hundreds place of all the numbers. The number with the smallest digit in the hundreds place is the smallest number.

Step 2: The next greater digit placed at the hundreds place is the next number and so on.

The order of the numbers is marked as given below.

629,	173,	805,	467
3	1	4	2

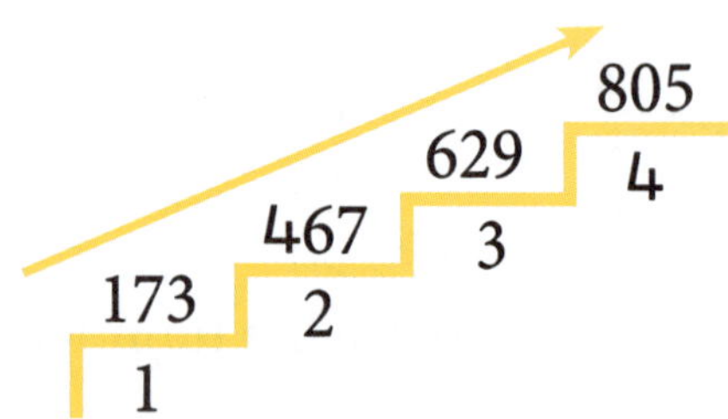

Hence, the ascending order of these numbers is:

173, 467, 629, 805

Example 4: Arrange the numbers in descending order.

295, 876, 531, 408

Solution:

Step 1: Check the digits placed at the hundreds place of all the numbers. The number with the greatest digit placed at the hundreds place is the greatest number.

Step 2: The next smaller digit at the hundreds place is the next number and so on.

The order of the numbers is marked as given below.

295,	876,	531,	408
4	1	2	3

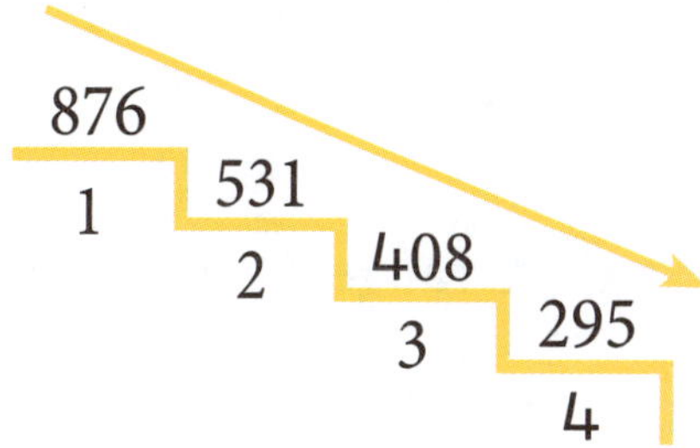

Hence, the descending order of these numbers is:

876, 531, 408, 295

NOTE

1. In ascending order in periods of 10, add 1 to the digit in the tens position.
2. In descending order in periods of 10, subtract 1 from the digit in the tens position.

Ordering Numbers in 10s

Let us now count numbers in periods of 10. In this case, we skip 10 numbers every time. That means, there is a gap of 10 numbers between any two numbers.

The following numbers have been arranged in periods of 10 in ascending order.

Complete the patterns.

a. 120, 130, 140, 150, 160, 170, ______, ______, ______, ______, ______

b. 310, 320, 330, 340, 350, 360, ______, ______, ______, ______, ______

c. 550, 560, 570, 580, 590, 600, ______, ______, ______, ______, ______

The following numbers have been arranged in periods of 10 in descending order.

Complete the patterns.

a. 490, 480, 470, 460, 450, 440, ______, ______, ______, ______, ______

b. 580, 570, 560, 550, 540, 530, ______, ______, ______, ______, ______

c. 850, 840, 830, 820, 810, 800, ______, ______, ______, ______, ______

We can also arrange numbers in ascending or descending order in periods of 100. For ascending order, add 1 to the digit in the hundreds position. For descending order, subtract 1 from the digit in the hundreds position.

EXERCISE 4E

1. **Arrange the numbers in the ascending order.**
   a. 349, 127, 805, 623 ________, ________, ________, ________
   b. 908, 673, 158, 691 ________, ________, ________, ________
2. **Arrange the numbers in the descending order.**
   a. 573, 189, 640, 257 ________, ________, ________, ________
   b. 329, 746, 150, 928 ________, ________, ________, ________
3. **Complete the patterns.**
   a. 540, 550, ________, ________, ________, ________
   b. 376, 476, ________, ________, ________, ________
   c. 780, 770, ________, ________, ________, ________
   d. 940, 930, ________, ________, ________, ________

BEFORE, AFTER, IN-BETWEEN

Let us understand the difference between

- before and just before
- after and just after

Sam and his friends are standing in a line.

1. Radhika is standing **just before** Sam.

   Nick, Khilee, Kavya and Radhika are standing **before** Sam.

   Now, consider the following sequence of numbers.

   125, 126, 127, 128, 129, 130

   129 comes **just before** 130 and

   125, 126, 127, 128, 129 come **before** 130.

NOTE

To find the number just before, subtract 1 from the digit in the ones position.

To find the number just after, add 1 to the digit in the ones position.

2. Khilee is standing **just after** Nick.

Khilee, Kavya, Radhika and Sam are standing **after** Nick.

Hence, in the sequence of numbers given below:

125, 126, 127, 128, 129, 130

126 comes **just after** 125 and 126, 127, 128, 129, 130 come **after** 125.

3. Kavya is standing in-between Khilee and Radhika. Similarly, Radhika is standing in-between Kavya and Sam.

Hence, in the sequence of numbers given below:

125, 126, 127, 128, 129, 130

126 comes in-between 125 and 127.

Let us practise a few problems.

Example 5: Write the number that comes just before 468.

a. ______, 468

467, 468

Example 6: Write the number that comes just after 333.

b. 333, ______

333, 334

Example 7: Write the numbers that come in-between the given numbers.

a. 394, ______, 396

394, 395, 396

b. 721, ______, ______, 724

721, 722, 723, 724

EXERCISE 4F

1. **Write the number that comes just after the given number.**

a. 135, ______ b. 623, ______ c. 467, ______ d. 854, ______

2. **Write the number that comes just before the given number.**

a. ______, 275 b. ______, 498 c. ______, 614 d. ______, 801

3. **Write the numbers that come in-between the given numbers.**

a. 234, ______, 236 b. 721, ______, 723

c. 946, ______, 948 d. 669, ______, ______, 672

4. **Write two numbers that come after 445.** ______________

5. **Write three numbers that come before 871.** ______________

FORMATION OF NUMBERS

Numbers can be formed by arranging the given digits in the ascending order or descending order.

Example 8: Arrange the digits 5, 0 and 7 to form the greatest number and the smallest number.

The greatest number formed using the digits 5, 0 and 7 is 750.

The smallest number formed using the digits 5, 0 and 7 is 507.

Go Easy!

Formation of smallest number with 0 as one of the digits

- If 0 is one of the digits in a 3-digit number, do not place it at the hundreds position. If 0 is placed at the hundreds position, the number becomes a 2-digit number. In that case, always place 0 at the tens position.
- Similarly, to form a 2-digit number, do not place 0 at the tens position. Always place it at the ones position. Otherwise, it will become a 1-digit number.

Exercise 4G

Arrange the following digits to form the greatest and the smallest numbers.

	Digits	Greatest Number	Smallest Number
1.	3 and 8	______	______
2.	1 and 5	______	______
3.	2, 0 and 9	______	______
4.	4, 6 and 7	______	______

CROSSWORD

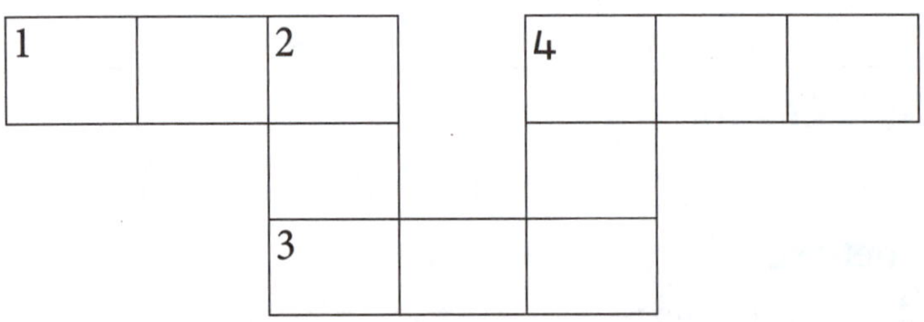

Across

1. I am 1 more than 627.
3. I am 10 more than 572.
4. I am 100 less than 891.

Down

2. I have 8 in my hundreds position, 9 in my tens position and 5 in my ones position.
4. I have 7 in my hundreds position, 3 in my tens position and 2 in my ones position.

Mental Maths

1. _______ is the smallest 4-digit number. Write its number name. ________________
2. _______ is the place value of 6 in 536. What is the face value of 3? _______
3. Place value and face value of a digit are the same when the digit is placed at the _______ position.
4. Expanded form of 391 is ________________.
5. Fill > or < in the blank. 459 _______ 495.
6. The greatest number formed using the digits 8, 0 and 9 is _______.

Maths Lab Activity

21 CS Information Literacy, Life Skills EL

Aim: To find the smallest number out of a given set of numbers

Materials required: Notebook and pen

Procedure:

1. Take a walk in your locality with a notebook and a pen and observe the number plates of 10 cars.
2. Now, note down the last three digits of all the numbers on the number plates of these cars. Write these numbers in an ascending order.
3. Which is the smallest number out of these numbers?

Conclusion: We learnt how different 3-digit numbers can be compared in real life.

Concept Map

Numbers up to 1000

- 3-digit numbers on the number line
- Place value and face value
- Expanded form of 3-digit numbers
- Comparing 3-digit numbers
- Ascending order and descending order
- Formation of numbers

Key Concepts

- Numbers up to 1000 can be represented on the number line.
- **Ordering numbers in 10s:** We can arrange the numbers with periods of 10 in ascending or descending order.
- Numbers can be formed by arranging the given digits in ascending or descending order.

A. Fill in the blanks.

1. 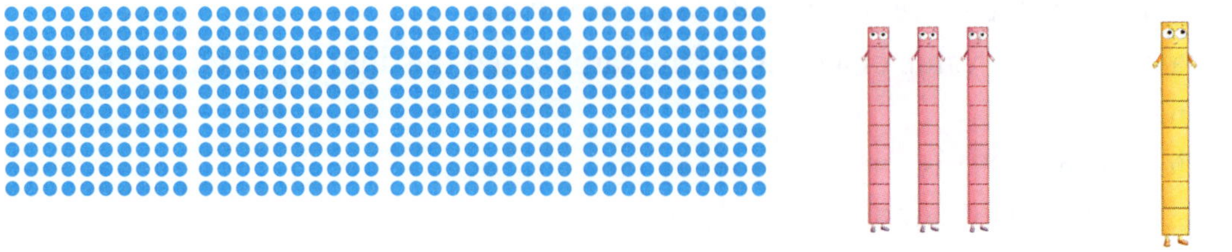

____ hundreds ____ tens ____ ones

Number name = ______________________________

2. 

____ hundreds ____ tens ____ ones

Number name = ______________________________

3. ______________________________ is the greatest 3-digit number.
4. The short form of 600 + 50 + 3 is ______________________________.
5. The greatest number formed using the digits 3, 9 and 0 is

   ______________________________.
6. The ascending order of 821, 811, 819, 919 and 812 is

   ______________________________.

B. Write the missing numbers on the number line given below.

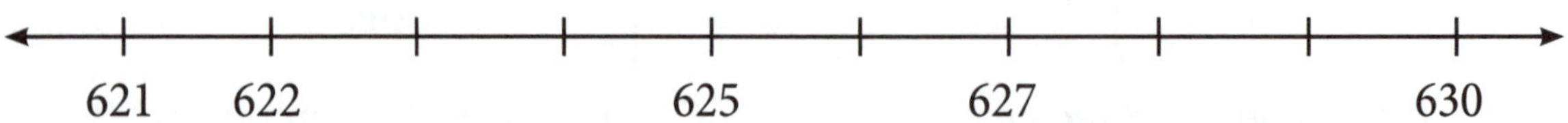

C. The students decorated the school premises with 125 balloons at the school fete.

1. Write the number name of 125. ______________________
2. Write the expanded form of 125. ______________________
3. Write the place value and face value of 2 in 125.

   ____

D. Write T for true and F for false.

1. 771 is greater than 779. ☐
2. 421 is the smallest 3-digit number formed using the digits 1, 2 and 4. ☐
3. The numeral for five hundred twenty-nine is 529. ☐
4. The face value of 8 in 180 is 80. ☐
5. The numbers 391, 310, 317, 371 are in descending order. ☐

E. Compare the numbers and put the correct sign (> or <).

1. 431 ☐ 485
2. 221 ☐ 212
3. 398 ☐ 432
4. 817 ☐ 877

F. Complete the patterns.

1. 510, 610, ________, ________, ________

2. 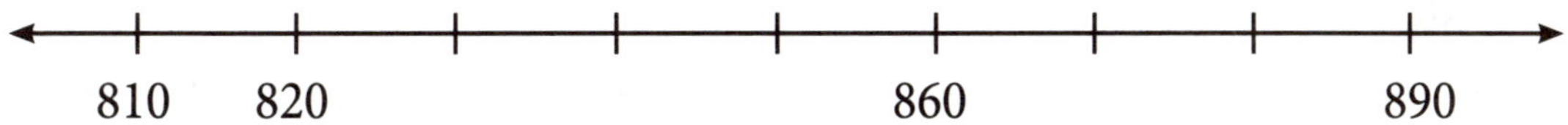

G. Write the number that comes just after 455. ________

H. Write four numbers that come after 237 ________, ________, ________ **and** ________.

I. Write any four numbers that come in-between 984 and 999.

________, ________, ________ **and** ________.

J. Write the short form of 200 + 10 + 1. Write its number name.

____

SKILL UP!

A. 21 CS Critical Thinking, Information Literacy | EL | AI | STEAM CHALLENGE

Few children can cut cards from the pastel sheet and write 100 on 9 cards and 10 on 9 more cards. They should also write digits from 1 to 9 on another set of 9 cards. Now, they can ask each other to form numbers like 453, 129, 390, 800, etc. To form 453, we can use cards as given below.

100	100	100	100	10	10	10	10	10	3

To form 129, we can use cards as given below.

100	10	10	9

Ask them to call aloud the number names of the numbers as well.

B. 21 CS Information Literacy, Media Literacy

Find the heights of some of the tallest buildings in the world. The heights should be 3-digit numbers.

(**Example:** Height of World Trade Center in New York, U.S.A. is 417 m.)

C. 21 CS Life Skills | CC Integration with Environmental Studies | HQ Harmony In The Self, Cooperation and Collaborative Living

6 CLEAN WATER AND SANITATION

13 CLIMATE ACTION

During floods in a village, the government provided 453 food packets and 589 water bottles to the villagers.

a. Write the number name for the number of food packets provided by the government.

b. Write the expanded form of the number of water bottles provided to the villagers.

D. 21 CS Critical Thinking

Who am I?

I'm a 3-digit number. I have 7 in my ones place. I have 5 in my tens place.

The digit at my hundreds place has 900 as the place value.

I am ____________________

SUSTAINABLE DEVELOPMENT GOALS

Question C is in line with SDG 2, SDG 6 and SDG 13. Many floods occur due to climate change. Floods affect clean drinking water and are responsible for bad sanitation. Climate change is the biggest factor that leads to floods. Only if climate change is under control, will fewer floods occur. Less floods mean less hunger (SDG 2) and better availability of clean water and sanitation (SDG 6).

WORKSHEET 4

21 CS Critical Thinking   HQ Knowing My Needs

3 GOOD HEALTH AND WELL-BEING

A fruit seller had the following quantity of fruits to sell in his shop.

670	**680**	**780**	**920**

1. Write the number names of the quantity of all the fruits in the shop.
   a. Apples ____________________
   b. Bananas ____________________
   c. Grapes ____________________
   d. Strawberries ____________________
2. Write the place value of all the digits in the quantity of grapes.

Digits	Place value
7	________
8	________
0	________

3. Which fruit was 10 more than apples in quantity? ____________
4. Which fruit was 100 less than grapes in quantity? ____________
5. The quantity of which fruit was the greatest? ____________
6. The quantity of which fruit was the least? ____________
7. Write the names of the fruits in the descending order, in terms of quantity.

   ____

It is very healthy to eat fresh fruit and vegetables. Do you eat them? ______

You should include them in your diet everyday!

5 Addition of Bigger Numbers

Learning Objectives

- To add bigger 2-digit numbers with regrouping
- To learn addition of 2- and 3-digit numbers without regrouping
- To add 3-digit numbers without regrouping
- To learn the correct placement of digits while adding numbers
- To solve word problems

Let's Get Started

21 CS Critical Thinking

John and Meg went to a school fete with their parents. There were swings, food joints, games, fun activities, etc. Solve the sums given below and find your answers in the fete scene. Draw arrows. One is done for you.

A

	T	O
	2	4
+	3	3
	5	7

B

	T	O
	4	9
+	1	2

C

	T	O
	6	1
+	3	6

D

	T	O
	9	8
+		1

E

	T	O
	2	5
	1	3
+	2	2

F

	T	O
	3	3
	2	1
+	1	8

G

	T	O
	1	1
	2	3
+	3	4

H

	T	O
	1	0
	1	1
+	4	9

ADDING BIGGER 2-DIGIT NUMBERS WITH REGROUPING

We have learnt addition of three 2-digit numbers in Chapter 2. Let us take some bigger 2-digit numbers and add them.

> **NOTE**
> Adding bigger 2-digit numbers results in 3-digit numbers.

Regrouping from Ones to Tens

Example 1: 88 + 74

When we add 88 and 74, we place them as shown below.

Solution:

	H	T	O
		8	8
+		7	4

Step 1:
First add the numbers in the ones column, that is, 8 + 4 = **12**

	H	T	O
		1	
		8	8
+		7	4
			2

Step 2:
Write '2' of 12 in the ones column. Carry forward '1' of 12 and write it above 8 in the tens column.

	H	T	O
		1	
		8	8
+		7	4
	1	6	2

Step 3:
Add 1 + 8 + 7 given in the tens column. We get 16. Write 6 of 16 in the tens column and '1' of 16 in the hundreds column.

So, 88 + 74 = **162**.

Example 2: Denny wants to distribute 55 toffees on his birthday and Rex wants to distribute 89 toffees. Find the total number of toffees that they want to distribute.

Solution: We will find the total number of toffees as shown below.

	H	T	O
		1	
		5	5
+		8	9
	1	4	4

Solve 5 + 9 given in the ones column. We get 14.

Write 4 in the ones column. Carry forward 1 to the tens column and write it above 5. Now, add 1 + 5 + 8. We get 14.

Write 4 of 14 in tens column and 1 of 14 in hundreds column.

So, 55 + 89 = **144**.

EXERCISE 5A

1. **Add the following.**

a.

	H	T	O
		5	8
+		7	1

b.

	H	T	O
		2	6
+		9	4

c.

	H	T	O
		7	4
+		3	7

d.

	H	T	O
		6	7
+		5	8

2. Aman has 66 coins and Raman has 55 coins. What is the total number of coins with them?

	H	T	O
+			

3. Kelly has 87 flowers in her garden. She plans to plant 50 more flowers. Find the total number of flowers Kelly plans to have.

	H	T	O
+			

ADDING 2- AND 3-DIGIT NUMBERS WITHOUT REGROUPING

Example 3: Add 123 + 64.

Solution: We place the digits in the hundreds, tens and ones columns.

	H	T	O
	1	2	3
+		6	4
	1	8	7

Ones column: 3 + 4 = 7
Tens column: 2 + 6 = 8
Hundreds column: There is no digit under 1, so we write 1 in the hundreds place.

So, 123 + 64 = **187**.

In this case, we get a 3-digit number after adding a 2- and a 3-digit number without carrying forward or regrouping.

COMMON ERRORS

	H	T	O
	1	2	0
+	4	9	

	H	T	O
	1	2	0
+		4	9

GO EASY!

It is easier to add 2-digit or 3-digit numbers by breaking them into hundreds, tens and ones. For example, 360 + 29 = 300 + 60 + 20 + 9 = 300 + 80 + 9 = 389

EXERCISE 5B

Add the following numbers.

1.

	H	T	O
	1	3	0
+		4	9

2.

	H	T	O
	1	2	3
+		3	1

3.

	H	T	O
	1	8	2
+		1	6

4.

	H	T	O
	2	0	4
+		7	3

ADDING 3-DIGIT NUMBERS WITHOUT REGROUPING

Let us see how we can add 3-digit numbers without carrying forward.

Adding Two 3-Digit Numbers

Example 4: Add 413 and 265.

Solution:

	H	T	O
	4	1	3
+	2	6	5
	6	7	8

Ones column:
$3 + 5 = 8$
Tens column:
$1 + 6 = 7$
Hundreds column:
$4 + 2 = 6$

So, $413 + 265 = 678$.

Adding Three 3-Digit Numbers

Example 5: Add 135, 212 and 321.

Solution:

	H	T	O
	1	3	5
	2	1	2
+	3	2	1
	6	6	8

Ones column:
$5 + 2 + 1 = 8$
Tens column:
$3 + 1 + 2 = 6$
Hundreds column:
$1 + 2 + 3 = 6$

So, $135 + 212 + 321 = 668$.

EXERCISE 5C

Add the following.

1.

	H	T	O
	2	1	4
+	7	5	3

2.

	H	T	O
	5	2	6
+	3	7	3

3.

	H	T	O
	7	5	2
	1	0	0
+	1	2	1

4.

	H	T	O
	6	4	3
	2	1	2
+	1	1	3

LEARNING CORRECT PLACEMENT OF DIGITS

Placing the digits correctly is very important while adding numbers that have different number of digits.

Examples:

1. Solve $218 + 31$.

	H	T	O
	2	1	8
+		3	1
	2	4	9

2. Solve $402 + 13 + 4$.

	H	T	O
	4	0	2
		1	3
+			4
	4	1	9

NOTE

Write the numbers as per their place value and then add.
Place the digits as given below:
Ones digits of all numbers in the ones column
Tens digits of all numbers in the tens column
Hundreds digits of all numbers in the hundreds column

EXERCISE 5D

Place the digits correctly and add.

1. 222 + 50
2. 317 + 41
3. 441 + 105 + 10
4. 112 + 13 + 2

	H	T	O
+			

WORD PROBLEMS

Addition is done when:

1. a quantity increases by a given amount
2. we need to find the sum or total

Let us look at the following examples.

> **NOTE**
> Look out for addition words in problems. They can give a clue to solve the problem. Addition words: Add, total, altogether, sum, plus, more, increase, etc.

Example 6: Ram has two storybooks. One book has 235 pages. The other book has 123 pages. What is the total number of pages in both the books?

Solution:

		H	T	O	
One book has =		2	3	5	pages
The other book has =	+	1	2	3	pages
		3	**5**	**8**	

So, the total number of pages in both the books is 358.

Example 7: There are 352 boys and 326 girls in a school. What is the total number of students in the school?

Solution:

		H	T	O
Boys =		3	5	2
Girls =	+	3	2	6
		6	**7**	**8**

So, the total number of students is 678.

EXERCISE 5E

1. 243 people went to see a football match on Monday and 125 people went to see the match on Tuesday. How many people went to see the match on Monday and Tuesday?

		H	T	O
Monday =				
Tuesday =	+			

_________ people went to see the match on Monday and Tuesday.

2. A bookshop has 240 English books and 154 Mathematics books. What is the total number of English and Mathematics books in the shop?

		H	T	O
English books =				
Mathematics books =	+			

There are ________ English and Mathematics books in the shop.

3. An ice cream vendor sold 248 ice creams on Saturday and 231 ice creams on Sunday. How many ice creams did he sell on these two days?

		H	T	O
Saturday =				
Sunday =	+			

The ice cream vendor sold ________ ice creams on these two days.

4. Ajoy has 134 red marbles, 264 green marbles and 300 blue marbles. What is the total number of marbles with Ajoy?

		H	T	O
Red marbles =				
Green marbles =				
Blue marbles =	+			

The total number of marbles with Ajoy is ________.

Mental Maths

1. I am a 3-digit number. I have 2 in my ones place, 5 in my tens place and 8 in my hundreds place. If I add 1 to my ones place, 1 to my tens place and 1 to my hundreds place, what will I become? ____________________
2. 242 + 100 = __________
3. 163 + 101 = __________
4. 901 + 98 = __________

CROSSWORD

Fill in the numbers in the squares below so that the sum of each side adds up to 150.

35	65	
		40
20	70	

Do you know?

We know that **plus** means to **add**.
'Eleven plus two' is 11 + 2 = **13** and
'Twelve plus one' = 12 + 1 = **13**
What do you observe?
The sum is 13 and there are 13 letters in both the phrases:
'Eleven plus two' and **'Twelve plus one'**.

Fun facts about the number 13!
Not so unlucky!

1. In Greek mythology, Zeus was the thirteenth god and the most powerful one.
2. The number 13 is significantly represented at the Winchester Mystery House in San Jose: 13 bathrooms, 13 steps in the staircases, etc.
3. In certain countries, such as Belgium, some employees get a "13th month" pay cheque. So it is lucky for them!
4. In Italy, 13 is considered as a very lucky number. The expression, *fare tredici* ("to do 13") means hit the jackpot.

Maths Lab Activity

21 CS Critical Thinking, Collaboration EL

Aim: To learn addition of 2- and 3-digit numbers using flashcards.

Materials required: Flashcards numbered 1, 10, 20, 50 and 100

Procedure:

100 | 50 | 20 | 10 | 1

1. Make the following flashcards.

   9 flashcards of 100 each — 100

   10 flashcards of 50 each — 50

   10 flashcards of 20 each — 20

   10 flashcards of 10 each — 10

   10 flashcards of 1 each — 1

2. Divide the whole class into 2 teams.
3. Let one team give a 2-digit and a 3-digit numbers to the other team. The other team must calculate the sum and represent it in the form of flashcards.
4. The two teams can do this turn by turn.

Concept Map

Addition of bigger numbers

- Addition of bigger 2-digit numbers with regrouping
- Addition of 2- and 3-digit numbers without regrouping
- Addition of 3-digit numbers without regrouping
- Word problems
  - sum
  - in all
  - total
  - altogether

Key Concepts

- We learnt,
  - addition of bigger 2-digit numbers with regrouping.
  - addition of 2- and 3-digit numbers without regrouping.
  - addition of 3-digit numbers without regrouping.
- **Word problems on addition:** Real-life situations where we need to understand the increase in quantities or amounts.

Chapter Revision

A. Choose the correct option.

1. 54 + 29 = [79] [84] [83]
2. 145 + 22 = [167] [293] [193]

B. Fill in the blanks.

1. 300 + 400 = ________
2. 245 + 10 = 10 + ________ = ________
3. Adding 20 to 500 gives __________.
4. 78 + 55 = __________
5. 310, 410, 510, ______, ______, ______
6. 300 + 50 in words is _______________.

C. Add the following.

1.

	H	T	O
	5	3	4
+	2	1	2

2.

	H	T	O
	9	3	2
+		4	3

3.

	T	O
	2	0
	1	5
+	1	2

4.

	T	O
	2	5
	1	7
+	4	3

5.

	H	T	O
	1	0	3
	2	1	5
+	3	4	0

6.

	H	T	O
	3	0	0
	2	0	0
+	4	0	0

D. Match the following.

Column A	Column B
1. 100 + 400	One hundred seventy
2. 150 + 20	Two hundred sixty-five
3. 220 + 45	Four hundred eighty
4. 350 + 130	Five hundred

E. Write T for true and F for false.

1. Adding two 3-digit numbers can give a 2-digit number. [ ]
2. The sum of 600 and 25 is 652. [ ]
3. The sum of 201 and 30 is an even number. [ ]
4. Consider the numbers:

   200, 400, 600 and 800

   The sum of 100 and 700 is the fourth number given above. [ ]

F. Solve the following word problems.

1. There are 250 tables and 122 chairs in a school. What is the total number of tables and chairs in the school?

	H	T	O
Tables =			
Chairs = +			

The total number of tables and chairs is ___________.

2. In a rose garden, there were 368 plants of red roses and 331 plants of pink roses. What is the total number of rose plants in the garden?

	H	T	O
Plants of red roses =			
Plants of pink roses – +			

The total number of rose plants is ___________.

3. A shopkeeper sold 12 dolls in first week and 39 dolls in the second week. Find the number of dolls he sold in both the weeks.

	T	O
Dolls sold in the first week =		
Dolls sold in the second week = +		

The number of dolls that he sold in both the weeks was ___________.

4. 525 students participated in the Republic Day celebrations of a school. 43 more students volunteered to participate. How many students participated altogether?

	H	T	O
Number of students participated =			
Number of volunteers = +			

Altogether, __________ students participated.

Skill Up!

A. 21 CS Critical Thinking, Life Skills

Visit your nearby stationery shop and ask the prices of a notebook, an eraser and a pencil. Note down the prices and find out how much would you have to pay if you buy

a. A pencil and an eraser
b. A notebook and an eraser
c. A notebook and a pencil
d. A notebook, a pencil and an eraser

B. 21 CS Information Literacy, Life Skills | CC Integration with Science | HQ Coexisting with Nature

In town A, there were 124 factories. In town B, there were 105 factories. These factories produce black smoke and pollute the air.

To clean the air, we need to stop the factories from producing black smoke. Find the total number of factories that should be stopped from producing smoke in both the towns altogether.

Do you think air is getting polluted to a great extent? What do you think should be done to clean the air around us?

C. 21 CS Critical Thinking

Which of the following add up to 987?

a. 567 + 420
b. 444 + 543
c. 900 + 88
d. 910 + 79

D. Find the missing digits.

	H	T	O
	2	4	__
	__	5	3
+	5	__	5
	8	9	9

Sustainable Development Goals

Question B is in line with SDG 12 Responsible Consumption and Production. While factories might be important for making things for people, they also pollute the environment. So, what can one do to stop pollution while keeping factories?

WORKSHEET 5

21 CS Critical Thinking AI

Solve the sums given in the balloons. Colour the balloons according to the given colour codes.

a.
```
  H T O
  2 1 4
+ 3 5 0
-------

```

b.
```
  H T O
  1 2 3
+ 4 0 5
-------

```

c.
```
  H T O
  1 0 4
+   2 5
-------

```

d.
```
  H T O
  1 0 3
+ 2 1 5
-------

```

e.
```
  H T O
  2 1 4
+ 1 5 0
-------

```

f.
```
  H T O
  4 0 6
+ 3 1 2
-------

```

g.
```
  H T O
  2 0 0
+ 3 0 1
-------

```

h.
```
  H T O
  2 1 1
+   4 7
-------

```

i.
```
  H T O
  5 7 2
+ 4 1 3
-------

```

j.
```
  H T O
  2 4 7
+ 3 1 0
-------

```

k.
```
  H T O
  9 1 4
+   2 3
-------

```

Colour codes

Colour all balloons whose sum is in-between:

a. 700 and 999 – Red

b. 500 and 700 – Pink

c. 100 and 500 – Blue

6 Subtraction of Bigger Numbers

Learning Objectives

- To learn subtraction of 1-, 2- and 3-digit numbers from 3-digit numbers (without regrouping)
- To learn the correct placement of digits while subtracting numbers
- To learn how to find missing digits in a subtraction problem
- To solve word problems

Let's Get Started

21 CS Critical Thinking, Information Literacy

We learnt subtraction of 2-digit numbers without borrowing in Class 1. Let us recall.

1. There were 29 children playing in a park. Out of them, 15 were girls. How many boys were there?

		T	O
Total number of children =		2	9
Number of girls =	−	1	5
Number of boys =		1	4

There were 14 boys.

2. Solve the following subtraction problems inside the clouds.

16 less than 39 is?

	T	O
	3	9
−	1	6

39 − 16 = ______

Take away 52 from 68.

	T	O
	6	8
−	5	2

68 − 52 = ______

48 minus 26 is?

	T	O
	4	8
−	2	6

48 − 26 = ______

SUBTRACTION OF BIGGER NUMBERS WITHOUT REGROUPING

Let us learn how to perform subtraction of

- 1- and 2-digit numbers from 3-digit numbers
- 3-digit numbers from 3-digit numbers

Subtraction of 1-Digit Numbers from 3-Digit Numbers

1-digit numbers are subtracted from 3-digit numbers in the same way as 1-digit numbers are subtracted from 2-digit numbers.

Example 1: Subtract 5 from 376.

Solution:

	H	T	O
	3	7	6
–			5
	3	**7**	**1**

So, 376 – 5 = 371.

Subtraction of 2-Digit Numbers from 3-Digit Numbers

For subtracting 2-digit numbers from 3-digit numbers, first subtract the ones digits, then the tens digits and finally retain the hundreds digit of the 3-digit number as it is.

Example 2: Out of 345 children in a class, 10 children were absent. How many children were present?

Solution:

		H	T	O
Total number of children =		3	4	5
Number of children absent =	–		1	0
				5

Step 1:

In the ones column, we subtract 0 from 5. We get 5 in the ones column.

	H	T	O
	3	4	5
–		1	0
		3	**5**

Step 2:

In the tens column, we subtract 1 from 4. We get 3 in the tens column.

	H	T	O
	3	4	5
–		1	0
	3	**3**	**5**

Step 3:

In the hundreds column, we have no digit to subtract from 3, hence we retain 3 in the hundreds column.

Therefore, 335 students were present.

More Examples:

1.

	H	T	O
	4	6	1
−		4	1
	4	2	0

2.

	H	T	O
	5	7	7
−		5	6
	5	2	1

Go Easy!

Write numbers according to their place values (one below the other) and then subtract.

PUZZLE!

Given that A = 444. Find the values of x, B and C as per the following.

a. x is a 2-digit number whose ones digit is equal to the tens digit.

b. C is a 3-digit number whose ones digit is 3.

c. A − x = C

d. A + x = B

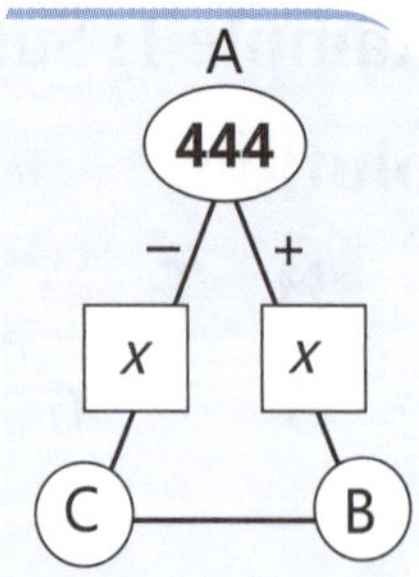

Subtraction of 3-Digit Numbers from 3-Digit Numbers

For subtracting 3-digit numbers from 3-digit numbers, first subtract the ones digits, then the tens digits and finally the hundreds digits.

Example 3: Radha bought some ice creams for ₹320. She gave ₹350 to the shopkeeper. How much money did she get in return from the shopkeeper?

Solution: We write this as a subtraction problem like

		H	T	O
Money given to the shopkeeper =		3	5	0
Cost of ice creams =	−	3	2	0
			3	0

The shopkeeper returned ₹30 to Radha.

More Examples:

1.

	H	T	O
	4	6	1
−	2	4	1
	2	2	0

2.

	H	T	O
	5	7	7
−	5	5	6
		2	1

Note

As we know, subtracting the number from itself gives the result as 0. If this happens in the hundreds column, we need not write 0 there.

3.

	H	T	O
	6	3	9
−	2	1	4
	4	2	5

4.

	H	T	O
	7	9	9
−	5	8	3
	2	1	6

COMMON ERRORS !

The bigger number should always be on top while subtracting

	H	T	O
	1	3	1
−	3	4	2

	H	T	O
	3	4	2
−	1	3	1

EXERCISE 6A

Subtract the following.

1.

	H	T	O
	9	8	8
−			3

2.

	H	T	O
	4	9	6
−			4

3.

	H	T	O
	8	5	7
−		4	6

4.

	H	T	O
	6	2	9
−		2	0

5.

	H	T	O
	2	9	8
−		3	7

6.

	H	T	O
	3	4	5
−		2	0

7.

	H	T	O
	4	6	9
−	1	1	7

8.

	H	T	O
	8	7	4
−	5	6	3

LEARNING CORRECT PLACEMENT OF DIGITS

Just like addition, we must also learn how to place the digits correctly before subtracting two numbers having different number of digits. Ones digits of both the numbers must be placed in the ones column (O), tens digits in the tens column (T) and hundreds digits in the hundreds column (H).

Example 4: Solve the following.

a. 355 – 35

	H	T	O
	3	5	5
−		3	5
	3	2	0

b. 467 – 5

	H	T	O
	4	6	7
−			5
	4	6	2

COMMON ERRORS !

Solve 187 – 25.

	H	T	O
	1	8	7
−	2	5	

	H	T	O
	1	8	7
−		2	5

Digits must be placed according to their place values.

EXERCISE 6B

Place the digits correctly and subtract.

1. 522 – 11
2. 767 – 25
3. 589 – 61
4. 299 – 34

	H	T	O
–			

MENTAL MATHS

1. Subtract 130 from 250. ____________
2. Subtract the smallest 3-digit number from 699. ____________
3. From 300, subtract the number that comes just after 199. ____________
4. ____________ + 10 = 810
5. 654 – 1 = ____________

DO YOU KNOW?

There are different methods of subtraction followed in different countries. For example, Austrian Method, American Method, Subtraction from left to right, which is unlike the subtraction method that we follow from right to left, non-vertical methods, etc.

FIND THE MISSING DIGITS

When some digits are missing in the subtraction problems, we can find them using the rules given below.

a. To find the digit in first row, add the digits in the second and the third rows.

b. To find the digit in the second row, subtract the digit in the third row from the digit in the first row.

Example 5: Find the missing digits.

a.

	H	T	O
	5	7	8
–	3	6	3
	2	1	5

To find the missing digits,
Ones column: 8 – 5 = **3**
Tens column: 7 – 1 = **6**
Hundreds column:
5 – 2 = **3**

b.

	H	T	O
	7	8	9
–	4	2	4
	3	6	5

To find the missing digits,
Ones column: 9 – 5 = **4**
Tens column: 2 + 6 = **8**
Hundreds column:
4 + 3 = **7**

EXERCISE 6C

Find the missing digits.

1.

	H	T	O
	8	9	4
−	—	—	—
	2	7	3

2.

	H	T	O
	9	1	3
−	—	—	—
	4	1	2

3.

	H	T	O
	—	7	—
−	3	—	4
	2	7	2

4.

	H	T	O
	—	—	4
−	6	5	—
	1	2	3

5.

	H	T	O
	7	8	6
−	—	—	1
	6	4	—

6.

	H	T	O
	8	5	9
−	3	4	—
	—	—	2

7.

	H	T	O
	4	8	8
−	3	—	1
	—	2	—

8.

	H	T	O
	—	—	9
−	2	1	1
	4	8	—

WORD PROBLEMS

Example 6: Niel planted 298 mango trees in his orchard. 124 trees died. How many trees were left in the orchard?

Solution:

		H	T	O
Total number of trees =		2	9	8
Numbers of trees that died =	−	1	2	4
		1	7	4

174 trees were left.

Example 7: Siddharth's book had 375 pages. He read 142 pages. How many pages are left to be read?

Solution:

		H	T	O
Total number of pages =		3	7	5
Pages read =	−	1	4	2
		2	3	3

233 pages are left to be read.

EXERCISE 6D

1. **A movie hall had 576 seats. 432 seats were occupied. How many seats were vacant?**

	H	T	O
Total number of seats =			
Number of seats occupied = −			

_______________ seats were vacant.

2. **Anisha had 783 apples growing in her orchard. She plucked 532 apples out of them. How many apples were left?**

	H	T	O
Total number of apples =			
Apples plucked by Anisha = −			

_______________ apples were left in the orchard.

3. **John had 398 marbles. He lost 25 marbles. How many marbles were left with him?**

	H	T	O
Total marbles =			
Marbles lost = −			

_______________ marbles were left with him.

4. **A bookshop had 963 books. 251 books got sold in one week. How many books were left in the shop?**

	H	T	O
Total number of books =			
Books sold = −			

_______________ books were left in the shop.

MATHS LAB ACTIVITY

21 CS Critical Thinking, Technology Literacy | EL | STEAM CHALLENGE

Aim: To solve subtraction problems using an abacus

Materials required: Abacus

Procedure: Follow the steps given below to solve subtraction problems using an abacus.

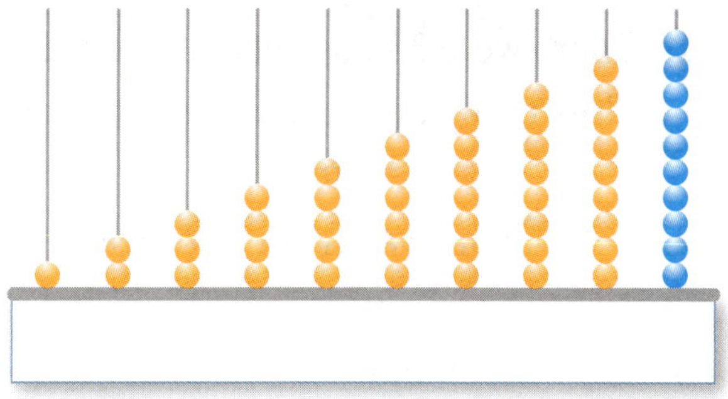

1. Let us solve 325 – 114.

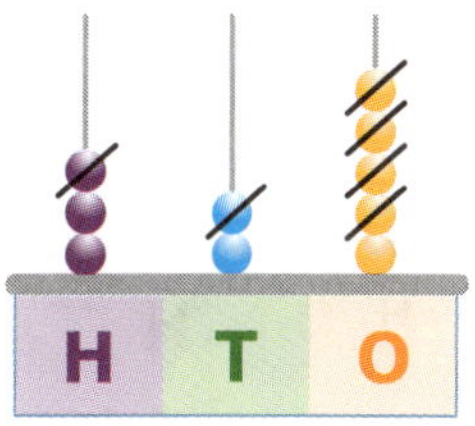

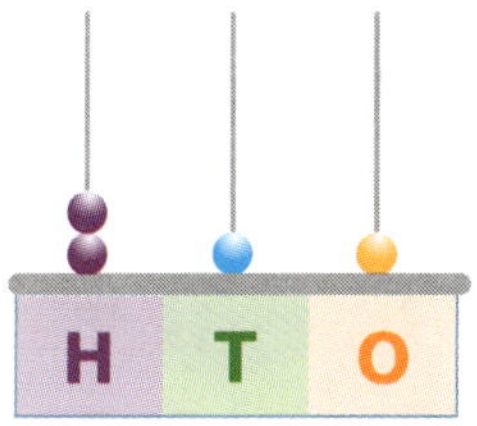

2. Take away 1 bead from the hundreds rod, 1 bead from the tens rod and 4 beads from the ones rod.

   So, 325 – 114 = **211**

3. Now try following subtraction problems using the abacus.

   a. 356 – 120   b. 458 – 52   c. 343 – 111   d. 569 – 21

CONCEPT MAP

Subtraction of bigger numbers

- Subtraction of 1-, 2- and 3-digit numbers from 3-digit numbers without regrouping
- Learning the correct placement of digits
- Finding the missing digits in a subtraction problem
- Word problems
  - minus
  - take away
  - by how much
  - difference
  - subtract
  - decrease
  - less than

KEY CONCEPTS

- We learnt the subtraction of 1-, 2- and 3-digit numbers from 3-digit numbers without regrouping
- **Word problems on subtraction:** This chapter involves word problems on subtraction with bigger numbers.

CHAPTER REVISION

A. Choose the correct answer.

1. There were 334 sweets in a box. Bobby distributed 112 sweets among his friends. How many sweets are left in the box?

   226   222   442   220

2. 456 taken away from 897 gives

   440   541   441   543

3. How much more is 999 than 865?

   143   140   130   134

B. Subtract the following.

1.

	H	T	O
	9	3	7
–	6	1	4

2.

	H	T	O
	8	6	3
–	5	2	0

3.

	H	T	O
	7	9	8
–		4	6

4.

	H	T	O
	6	8	9
–	4	2	9

C. Fill in the blanks.

1.

	H	T	O
	3	—	7
–	—	5	—
	2	0	7

2.

	H	T	O
	—	9	8
–	1	—	—
	3	7	4

3.

	H	T	O
	8	7	—
–	—	—	3
	8	2	0

D. Place the digits correctly and solve.

1. 654 – 44

	H	T	O
–			

2. 843 – 40

	H	T	O
–			

3. 635 – 31

	H	T	O
–			

E. Solve the following word problems.

1. 455 children sat for an examination. 442 children passed the examination. How many children did not pass the examination?

   ____________ children did not pass the examination.

2. Mrs Pinto baked 245 biscuits. She sold 135 of them. How many biscuits are left?

   __________ biscuits are left.

SKILL UP!

A. 21 CS Critical Thinking, Information Literacy

Take the 2022 calendar. Count the number of days in every month. Add all of them. How many days are there in the whole year?

1. The total number of days is in between:

   a. 100 to 200 b. 200 to 300 c. 300 to 400 d. 400 to 500

2. How many less days than 999 are there in the whole year?

B. 21 CS Information Literacy, Life Skills HQ Living in an Interconnected Society

4 QUALITY EDUCATION

The government started free education for students whose parents could not pay the school fee. 342 students joined the school. When the school started evening classes, the number of students increased to 978.

1. How many more students joined the school after the evening classes started?
2. Should the government provide free education to those students whose parents can't pay the school fee?

SUSTAINABLE DEVELOPMENT GOALS

Question B is in line with SDG 4 Quality Education. Everyone should have the opportunity to learn. Each one of us should take part in providing this opportunity. If you are able to go to school, it is a blessing. Only after you get quality education, then only will you be able to help yourself, others, your country, and the entire world. Think about those children who are unable to go to school. What can you do for them?

WORKSHEET 6

21 CS Critical Thinking

Look at the heights of these sunflowers and answer the questions that follow.

1. How much taller is Sunflower A than Sunflower B? ____________ units
2. How much taller is Sunflower B than Sunflower C? ____________ units
3. If Sunflower D grows to be the same height as Sunflower A, how many more units will it need to grow? ____________ units
4. What is the difference in the height between Sunflower D and Sunflower E? ____________ units
5. How much shorter is Sunflower E than Sunflower B? ____________ units

Reasoning Worksheet 1

1. A car parking area outside a shopping complex can accommodate 80 cars. Which of the following is true for car accommodation?

   a. 140 cars b. 81 cars c. 71 cars d. 95 cars

2. Anu collected (294 + 105) fruit stickers. Bill collected (300 + 99) fruit stickers. Which of these are true?

   a. Anu has more stickers.
   b. The sum of stickers with Anu and Bill is 798.
   c. Bill has more stickers.
   d. Anu and Bill have equal number of stickers.

3. Write the 3-digit number using the following clues.
   - The ones digit is 7.
   - When 155 is subtracted from the number, the result is 42.

	H	T	O
−			

   a. 197 b. 179 c. 113 d. 117

4. A train has (130 + 157) seats. How many people can sit in the train?

   a. 400 b. 300 c. 280 d. 287

5. I have ₹$\begin{array}{r} 785 \\ -\,510 \\ \hline \end{array}$. What can be the price/prices of the dress that I can afford to buy?

   a. ₹250 b. ₹300 c. ₹375 d. ₹200

6. Given that each  = 100,

   each  = 10 and

   each  = 1

   Given below is the appropriate representation of which 3-digit number?

   a. 285 b. 295 c. 293 d. 290

7 Multiplication

Learning Objectives

- To solve repeated addition in a shorter time by using multiplication
- To learn the terms used in multiplication
- To learn multiplication tables of 1, 2, 3, 4, 5 and 10
- To understand multiplication on the number line
- To learn horizontal and vertical methods of multiplication
- To learn multiplication of 2- and 3-digit numbers with 1-digit numbers without regrouping
- To learn multiplication of 2-digit numbers with 1-digit numbers with regrouping
- To solve word problems

Let's Get Started

21 CS Critical Thinking, Information Literacy

The maths teacher gave a few multiplication problems to three students. Each student was supposed to find the product of two problems.

1. How many problems were solved by the students?
2. Can we use repeated addition to solve them?

Let us find out.

Number of students = 3

Number of problems to be solved by each student = 2

This can be written as:

Total number of problems = $2 + 2 + 2 = 3 \times 2 = \mathbf{6}$

Hence, the students solved a total of 6 multiplication problems.

WHAT IS MULTIPLICATION?

Whenever a quantity increases, we either add or multiply.

When a number increases by a certain amount, we add, but **when the same number is added over and over, we multiply.**

> × is the symbol of multiplication.

Example: 3 + 3 + 3 = **9**. We can say that 3 **times** 3 is 9.

The multiplication statement for this repeated addition is written as 3 × 3 = 9 (Product).

> **NOTE**
>
> To find the product means to multiply.
>
> The word 'times' refers to multiplication.

MULTIPLICATION AS REPEATED ADDITION

As we learned earlier, multiplication is also referred to as repeated addition. When we need to add the same number to itself a number of times, we can calculate it faster using multiplication.

Consider 3 groups of stars. Each group contains 6 stars.

Number of groups = 3

Number of stars in each group = 6

Therefore, 3 × 6 = **18**.

EXERCISE 7A

1. **Fill in the blanks and write the multiplication statements.**

a.  = ______ × ______ = ______

b. 

= ______________ × ______________ = ______________

2. **Write the multiplication statements for the following repeated additions.**

a. 3 + 3 + 3 + 3 + 3 + 3 + 3 = ______ × ______ = ______

b. 7 + 7 + 7 + 7 = ______ × ______ = ______

c. 4 + 4 + 4 + 4 + 4 + 4 = ______ × ______ = ______

d. 9 + 9 + 9 = ______ × ______ = ______

3. Match the pictures in Column A with the multiplication facts in Column B. Also, solve the multiplication problems.

	Column A	Column B
a.		$4 \times 8 =$ ____
b.		$9 \times 3 =$ ____
c.		$4 \times 5 =$ ____
d.		$3 \times 6 =$ ____

TERMS USED IN MULTIPLICATION

A multiplication statement consists of three numbers.

Two numbers are multiplied to give a **product**.

The two numbers being multiplied are called the **multiplier** and the **multiplicand**.

Example:

3	×	2	=	6
↓		↓		↓
Multiplier (or Multiplicand)		Multiplicand (or Multiplier)		Product

NOTE

1. In a multiplication statement, the order of the numbers being multiplied does not change the product.

   $$2 \times 1 = 2, 1 \times 2 = 2$$

2. If a number is multiplied with 1, the product is the number itself.

   $$2 \times 1 = 2, 8 \times 1 = 8$$

3. If a number is multiplied with 0, the product becomes 0.

   $$3 \times 0 = 0, 7 \times 0 = 0$$

MULTIPLICATION TABLES

Table of 1

Let us make the table of 1 by counting the number of lollipops in each row.

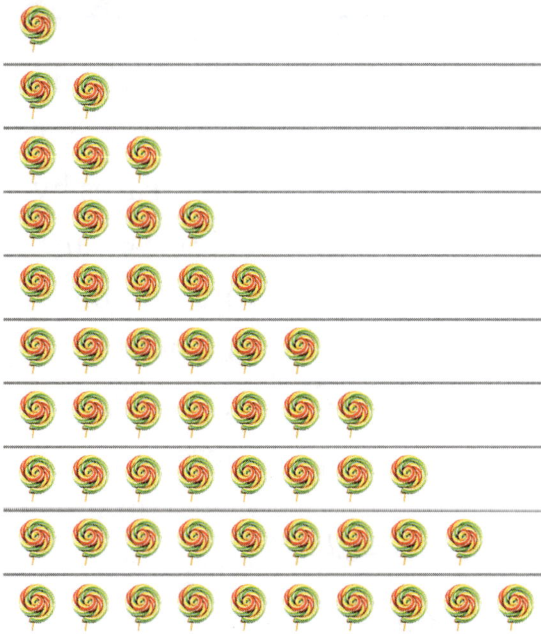

(1 lollipop)	$1 \times 1 = \mathbf{1}$
(2 lollipops)	$2 \times 1 = \mathbf{2}$
(3 lollipops)	$3 \times 1 = \mathbf{3}$
(4 lollipops)	$4 \times 1 = \mathbf{4}$
(5 lollipops)	$5 \times 1 = \mathbf{5}$
(6 lollipops)	$6 \times 1 = \mathbf{6}$
(7 lollipops)	$7 \times 1 = \mathbf{7}$
(8 lollipops)	$8 \times 1 = \mathbf{8}$
(9 lollipops)	$9 \times 1 = \mathbf{9}$
(10 lollipops)	$10 \times 1 = \mathbf{10}$

When we add 1 to a number, it increases by 1. So, we can form a table of 1, where the product increases by 1 every time.

NOTE

$1 \times 5 = \mathbf{5}$ is read as:

1 multiplied by 5 is equal to 5.

Table of 2

Let us make the table of 2 by counting twin babies in each row.

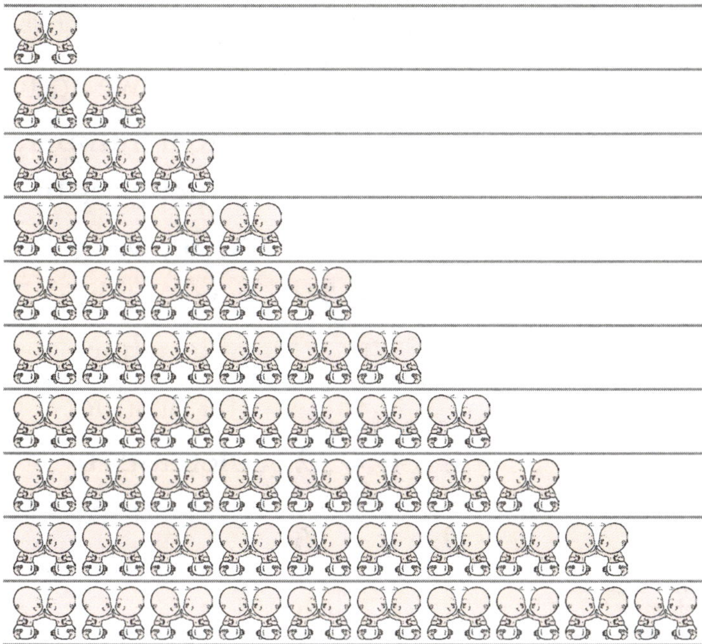

(1 pair of twins)	$1 \times 2 = \mathbf{2}$
(2 pairs of twins)	$2 \times 2 = \mathbf{4}$
(3 pairs of twins)	$3 \times 2 = \mathbf{6}$
(4 pairs of twins)	$4 \times 2 = \mathbf{8}$
(5 pairs of twins)	$5 \times 2 = \mathbf{10}$
(6 pairs of twins)	$6 \times 2 = \mathbf{12}$
(7 pairs of twins)	$7 \times 2 = \mathbf{14}$
(8 pairs of twins)	$8 \times 2 = \mathbf{16}$
(9 pairs of twins)	$9 \times 2 = \mathbf{18}$
(10 pairs of twins)	$10 \times 2 = \mathbf{20}$

When we add 2 to a number, it increases by 2. So, we can form a table of 2, where the product increases by 2 every time.

NOTE

The products in the table of 2 end with 0, 2, 4, 6 or 8.

Table of 3

Count the total number of wheels in the tricycles in each row to make the table of 3.

	1 × 3 = **3**
	2 × 3 = **6**
	3 × 3 = **9**
	4 × 3 = **12**
	5 × 3 = **15**
	6 × 3 = **18**
	7 × 3 = **21**
	8 × 3 = **24**
	9 × 3 = **27**
	10 × 3 = **30**

When we add 3 to a number, it increases by 3. So, we can form a table of 3, where the product increases by 3 every time.

Table of 4

Count the mathematical symbols in each row and make the table of 4.

[+ − × =]	1 × 4 = **4**
[+ − × =] [+ − × =]	2 × 4 = **8**
[+ − × =] [+ − × =] [+ − × =]	3 × 4 = **12**
[+ − × =] [+ − × =] [+ − × =] [+ − × =]	4 × 4 = **16**
[+ − × =] [+ − × =] [+ − × =] [+ − × =] [+ − × =]	5 × 4 = **20**
[+ − × =] [+ − × =] [+ − × =] [+ − × =] [+ − × =] [+ − × =]	6 × 4 = **24**
[+ − × =] [+ − × =] [+ − × =] [+ − × =] [+ − × =] [+ − × =] [+ − × =]	7 × 4 = **28**
[+ − × =] [+ − × =] [+ − × =] [+ − × =] [+ − × =] [+ − × =] [+ − × =] [+ − × =]	8 × 4 = **32**
[+ − × =] [+ − × =] [+ − × =] [+ − × =] [+ − × =] [+ − × =] [+ − × =] [+ − × =] [+ − × =]	9 × 4 = **36**
[+ − × =] [+ − × =] [+ − × =] [+ − × =] [+ − × =] [+ − × =] [+ − × =] [+ − × =] [+ − × =] [+ − × =]	10 × 4 = **40**

When we add 4 to a number, it increases by 4. So, we can form a table of 4, where the product increases by 4 every time.

Table of 5

Count the total number of dots on the dice in each row and make the table of 5.

	$1 \times 5 = \mathbf{5}$
	$2 \times 5 = \mathbf{10}$
	$3 \times 5 = \mathbf{15}$
	$4 \times 5 = \mathbf{20}$
	$5 \times 5 = \mathbf{25}$
	$6 \times 5 = \mathbf{30}$
	$7 \times 5 = \mathbf{35}$
	$8 \times 5 = \mathbf{40}$
	$9 \times 5 = \mathbf{45}$
	$10 \times 5 = \mathbf{50}$

DO YOU KNOW?

The dots on the opposite sides of a die always add up to 7.

1 + 6, 2 + 5, 3 + 4

Hence,
1 is always opposite to 6.
2 is always opposite to 5.
3 is always opposite to 4.

When we add 5 to a number, it increases by 5. So, we can form a table of 5, where the product increases by 5 every time.

Table of 10

Count the number of colours shown in each row and make the table of 10.

	$1 \times 10 = \mathbf{10}$
	$2 \times 10 = \mathbf{20}$
	$3 \times 10 = \mathbf{30}$
	$4 \times 10 = \mathbf{40}$
	$5 \times 10 = \mathbf{50}$
	$6 \times 10 = \mathbf{60}$
	$7 \times 10 = \mathbf{70}$
	$8 \times 10 = \mathbf{80}$
	$9 \times 10 = \mathbf{90}$
	$10 \times 10 = \mathbf{100}$

When we add 10 to a number, it increases by 10. So, we can form a table of 10, where the product increases by 10 every time.

Exercise 7B

1. **Learn the multiplication tables of 1, 2, 3, 4, 5 and 10 and write them in your notebook.**

2. **Complete the following.**

a. $3 \times 2 =$ ______ $\times 3$	b. $5 \times 2 =$ ______ $\times 5$	c. $2 \times 1 =$ ______
d. $4 \times 4 =$ ______	e. $6 \times 10 =$ ______	f. $5 \times 5 =$ ______
g. $7 \times 5 =$ ______	h. $0 \times 2 =$ ______	i. $9 \times 4 =$ ______
j. $1 \times 0 =$ ______	k. $8 \times 3 =$ ______	l. $8 \times 4 =$ ______

m. $2 \times 10 = 10 \times 2 =$ ______ n. $4 \times 5 = 5 \times 4 =$ ______

o. $3 \times 4 = 4 \times 3 =$ ______

3. **Fill in the blanks.**

   a. In $2 \times 5 = 10$,

   The multiplier is ________

   The multiplicand is ________

   The product is ________

   b. In $7 \times 5 = 35$,

   The multiplier is ________

   The multiplicand is ________

   The product is ________

PUZZLE!

Pick up a die.

1. Find out how many dots are there opposite to five dots.
   ____
2. Multiply the answer of the above question by 3. What do you get? __________

NUMBER LINE

A number line represents numbers in order. As we move to the right, the numbers increase and as we move to the left, the numbers decrease.
Let us learn the multiplication tables using number line.

Table of 1 on a number line is shown below:

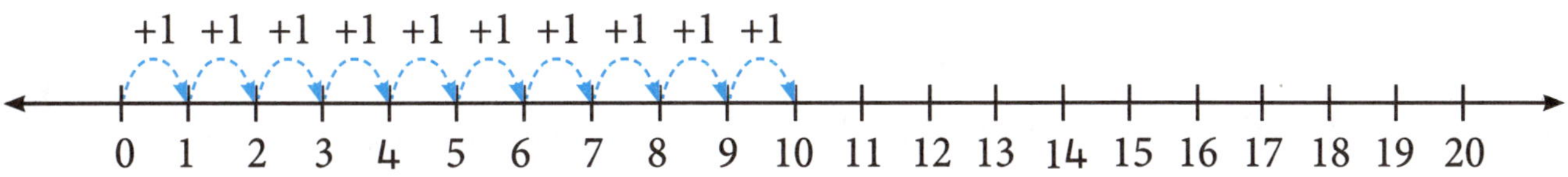

In the table of 1, the numbers increase by 1 every time. Look at the jumps of 1.

Table of 2 on a number line is shown below:

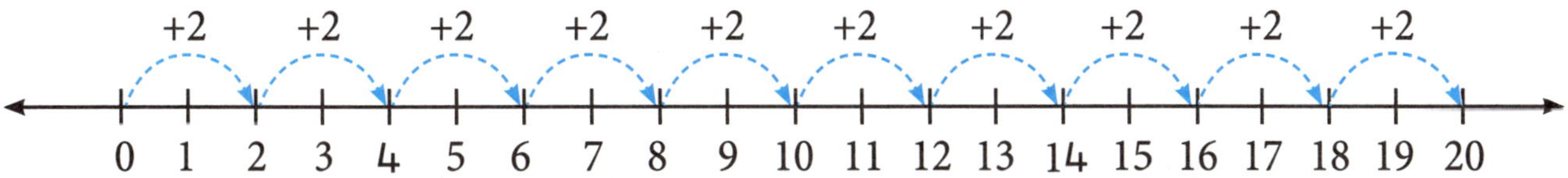

In the table of 2, the numbers increase by 2 every time. Look at the jumps of 2.

Table of 3 on a number line is shown below:

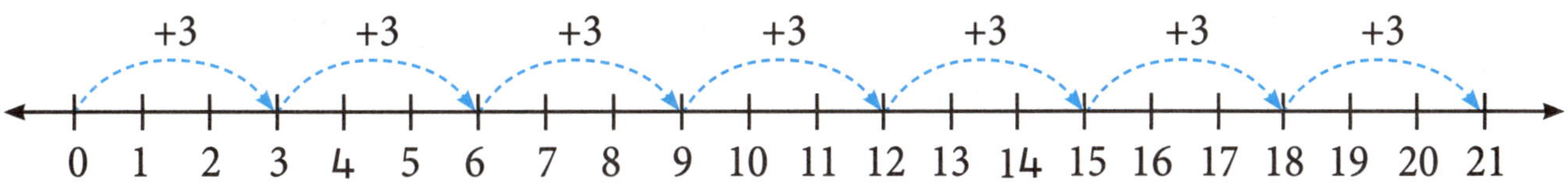

In the table of 3, the numbers increase by 3 every time. Look at the jumps of 3.

Table of 4 on a number line is shown below:

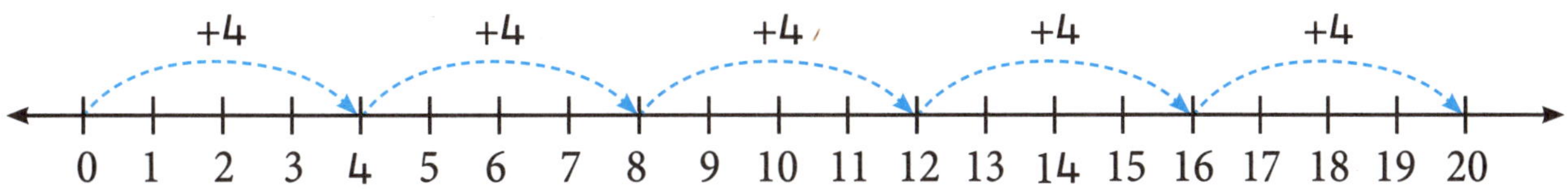

In the table of 4, the numbers increase by 4 every time. Look at the jumps of 4.

Table of 5 on a number line is shown below:

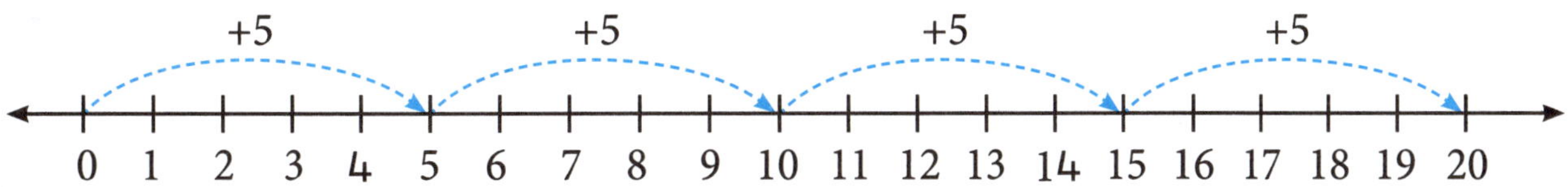

In the table of 5, the numbers increase by 5 every time. Look at the jumps of 5.

Table of 10 on a number line is shown below:

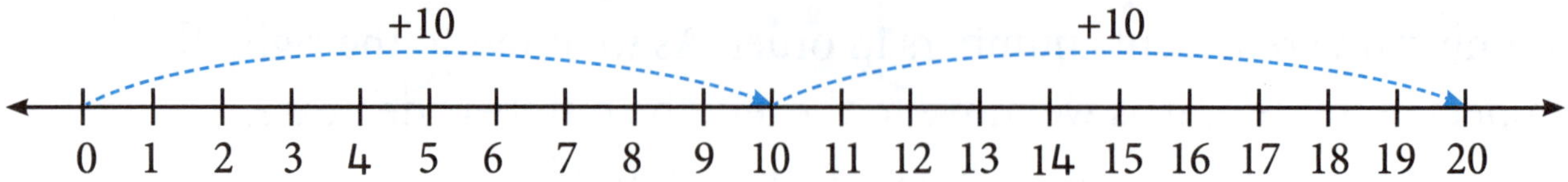

In the table of 10, the numbers increase by 10 every time. Look at the jumps of 10.

DOUBLES

Two times any number **doubles** the number.

Bobby ate 3 doughnuts. He wants to eat double the number of doughnuts. This means, he wants to eat 3 more doughnuts, that is, 3 + 3 = 6 doughnuts. How can we find the double of a number? We can find the double of a number by

- multiplying it by 2, or
- adding the number to itself.

Examples:

1. Write the double of 3.
   a. 3 × 2 = **6** or
   b. 3 + 3 = **6**

   This means double of 3 is 6.

2. Write the double of 10.
   a. 10 × 2 = **20** or
   b. 10 + 10 = **20**

   This means double of 10 is 20.

EXERCISE 7C

1. Multiply the given numbers using a number line and write the answer.

a. 2 × 5 = ______

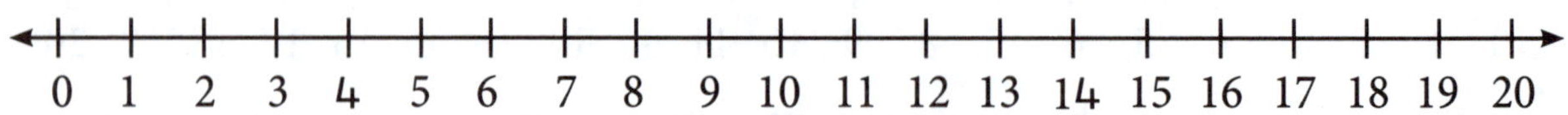

b. 4 × 3 = ______

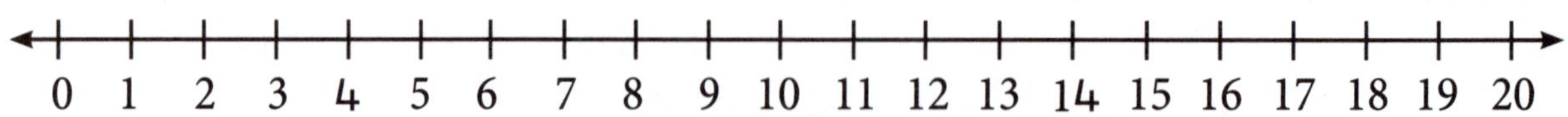

2. Find the double of:

a. 7 b. 5 c. 26 d. 330

HORIZONTAL AND VERTICAL METHODS OF MULTIPLICATION

Numbers can be multiplied using the horizontal method and vertical method. Both the methods are shown below.

Horizontal method	Vertical method
$4 \times 5 = \mathbf{20}$, $7 \times 10 = \mathbf{70}$	$\begin{array}{rcc} & T & O \\ & & 4 \\ \times & & 5 \\ \hline & 2 & 0 \end{array}$ $\begin{array}{rcc} & T & O \\ & 1 & 0 \\ \times & & 7 \\ \hline & 7 & 0 \end{array}$

MULTIPLICATION OF 2- AND 3-DIGIT NUMBERS WITH 1-DIGIT NUMBERS WITHOUT REGROUPING

Example 1: Multiply 13 × 2.

Solution: We know that, 13 is a 2-digit number and 2 is a 1-digit number.

Hence, we write the above multiplication statement as given below.

> **NOTE**
> We must remember the multiplication tables very well for finding the product of two numbers.

$$\begin{array}{rcc} & T & O \\ & 1 & 3 \\ \times & & 2 \\ \hline & & 6 \end{array}$$

Step 1: First, multiply 2 with 3 in the ones column, that is, 2 × 3 = **6**. Write 6 under 2 in the ones column.

$$\begin{array}{rcc} & T & O \\ & 1 & 3 \\ \times & & 2 \\ \hline & 2 & 6 \end{array}$$

Step 2: Multiply 2 with 1 in the tens column, that is, 2 × 1 = **2**. Write 2 in the tens column before 6.

So, 13 × 2 = **26**.

Example 2: Multiply 123 × 2.

Solution: We know that 123 is a 3-digit number and 2 is a 1-digit number. Hence, we write the above multiplication statement as given below.

$$\begin{array}{rccc} & H & T & O \\ & 1 & 2 & 3 \\ \times & & & 2 \\ \hline & 2 & 4 & 6 \end{array}$$

Ones column: 2 × 3 = **6**

Tens column: 2 × 2 = **4**

Hundreds column: 2 × 1 = **2**

So, 123 × 2 = **246**.

Go Easy!

When we multiply a number with a number ending with 0, we can use a shorter method which is explained below.

Example: Multiply 30 × 2

30 has one 0, so we write 0 at the end of the answer. $30 \times 2 = \_\_0$

Now, multiply the other digits, 3 and 2, $3 \times 2 = 6$. So, we write 6 before 0.

That is, $30 \times 2 = \underline{6}0$

In the same way, $300 \times 2 = 600$, $400 \times 2 = 800$, $200 \times 5 = 1000$, etc.

Mental Maths

1. $200 \times 2 =$ ☐ 2. $50 \times 2 =$ ☐ 3. $40 \times 8 =$ ☐ 4. $30 \times 3 =$ ☐

Exercise 7D

Find the products.

1.

	T	O
		9
×		5

2.

	T	O
	1	0
×		5

3.

	T	O
	5	6
×		1

4.

	H	T	O
	4	3	0
×			2

MULTIPLICATION OF 2-DIGIT NUMBERS WITH 1-DIGIT NUMBERS WITH REGROUPING

Example 3: Multiply 26 × 3.

Solution: We can write the above multiplication statement as given below.

	T	O
	2	6
×		3

Step 1: First multiply 3 with 6 in the ones column.

$3 \times 6 = \mathbf{18}$

	T	O
	1	
	2	6
×		3
		8

Step 2: Write 8 of 18 in the ones column under 3 and carry forward 1 of 18. Write this 1 above 2 in the tens column.

	T	O
	1	
	2	6
×		3
	7	**8**

Step 3: Now, multiply 3 with 2 in the tens column.

3 × 2 = **6**. Add the carried forward 1 to 6.

6 + 1 = **7**. Write 7 in the tens column, before 8.

So, 26 × 3 = **78**.

Common Errors

	T	O
	1	
	1	7
×		2
	2	4

(Wrong)

	T	O
	1	
	1	7
×		2
	3	4

(Right)

Exercise 7E

Multiply the following.

1.

	T	O
	1	6
×		2

2.

	T	O
	2	8
×		3

3.

	T	O
	1	2
×		8

4.

	T	O
	3	7
×		2

5.

	T	O
	4	5
×		2

WORD PROBLEMS

In word problems, whenever the answer increases, we **add** or **multiply**.

- When the answer increases exactly by the number given in the question, we **add**.
- When the answer increases many times by the number given in the question, we **multiply**.
- When the value of one item is given and we need to find the value of more such items, we **multiply**.

Let us solve the following examples.

Example 4: One tricycle has 3 wheels. How many wheels are there in 5 such tricycles?

Solution: Number of wheels in 1 tricycle = 3

Number of wheels in 5 tricycles = 5 × 3 = **15**

There are 15 wheels in 5 tricycles.

Example 5: Anita sells 134 cakes in one day. How many cakes does she sell in 2 days?

Solution: Number of cakes sold in 1 day = 134

Number of cakes sold in 2 days = 134 × 2

She sells 268 cakes in 2 days.

	H	T	O
	1	3	4
×			2
	2	**6**	**8**

Exercise 7F

1. **In a classroom, 6 children sit in one row. How many children can sit in 3 rows?**

Number of children in 1 row = ☐

Number of children in 3 rows = ☐ × ☐

= ☐

☐ children can sit in 3 rows.

2. **One packet has 9 pieces of cookies in it. How many pieces of cookies are there in 5 such packets?**

Number of pieces in 1 packet = ☐

Number of pieces in 5 packets = ☐ × ☐

= ☐

☐ pieces of cookies are there in 5 packets.

3. **A shopkeeper sells 323 shirts in one month. How many shirts does he sell in two months?**

Number of shirts sold in 1 month = ☐

Number of shirts sold in 2 months = ☐ × ☐

= ☐

He sells ☐ shirts in 2 months.

4. **230 people can sit in one train. How many people can sit in 3 such trains?**

Number of people that can sit in 1 train = ☐

Number of people that can sit in 3 trains = ☐ × ☐

= ☐

☐ people can sit in 3 trains.

5. **A box of erasers costs ₹45. How much do 6 boxes of erasers cost?**

Cost of 1 box of erasers = ₹ ______

Cost of 6 boxes of erasers = ______ × ______

= ₹ ______

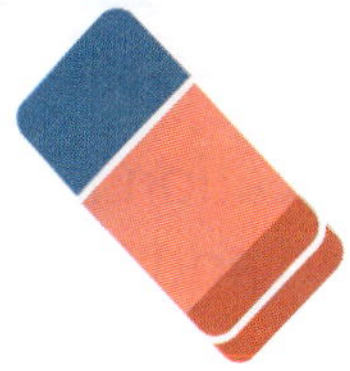

6 boxes of erasers will cost ₹ ______.

Mental Maths

1. 3 + 3 + 3 + 3 = _____ × 3 = _____.
2.  = 2 × 5 = _____.
3. Multiplier × Multiplicand = _______________
4. a. 4 × 0 = _____ b. 7 × 0 = _____
5. a. 6 × 1 = _____ b. 9 × 1 = _____
6. a. 3 × 5 = _____ b. 2 × 600 = _____
7. 1 × 2 = 2 × _____
8. Four multiplied by two is = 4 × _____ = _____
9. Double of 5 gives _____.
10. 10 × 2 gives _____.

Maths Lab Activity

21 CS Creativity and Innovation EL AI STEAM CHALLENGE

Aim: Construction of multiplication tables of 2, 3, 4 and 5 using ice cream sticks.

Materials required: Ice cream sticks

Procedure: To multiply 3 with 3

1. Put 3 sticks horizontally for the first number.

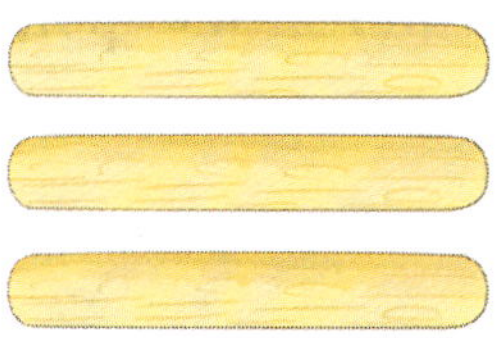

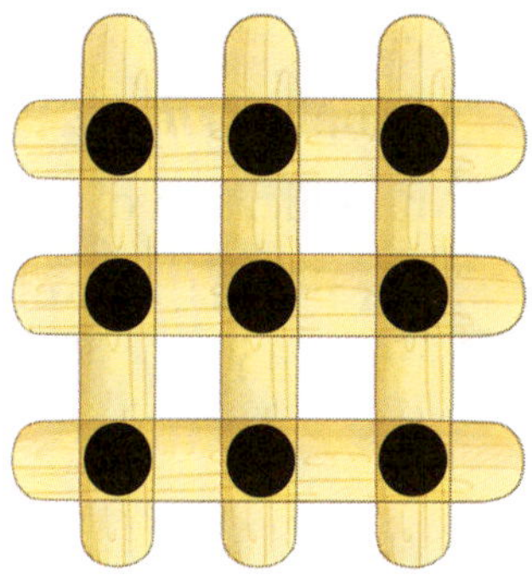

2. Now, put 3 sticks vertically, above the horizontal sticks, for the second number.
3. Now, count the number of points where the sticks meet (encircled in black).

The number of points is 9, so the answer is 3 × 3 = **9**.

Concept Map

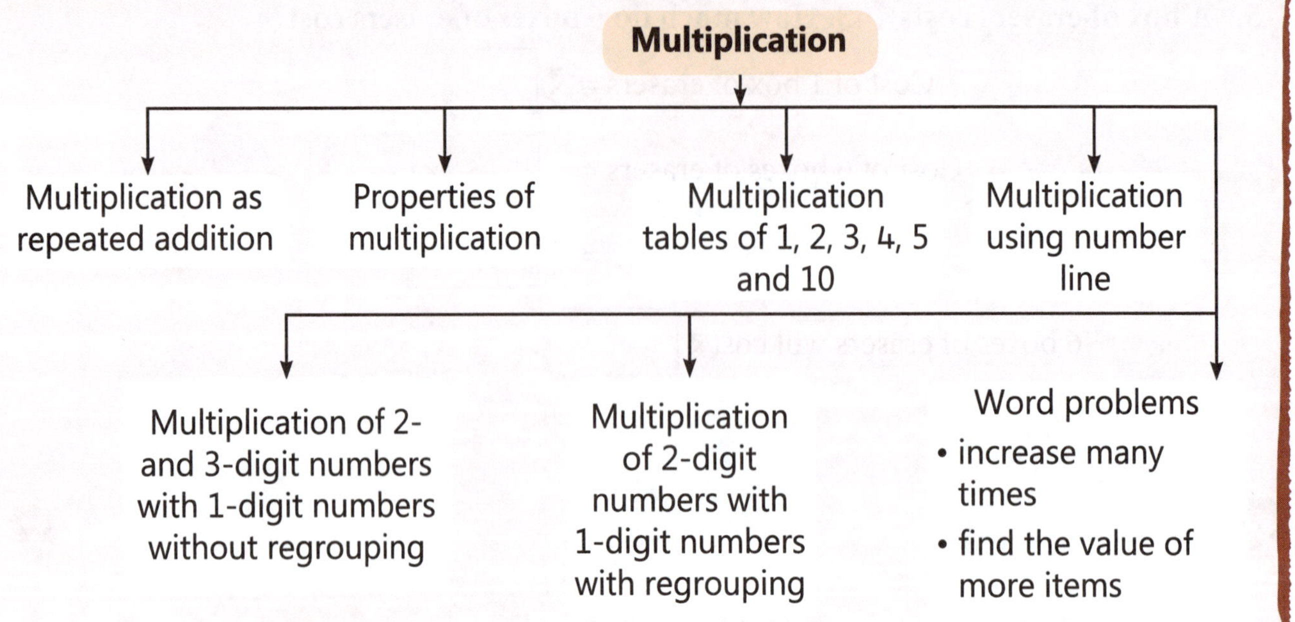

Key Concepts

- **Multiplication:** When the same number is added over and over, we multiply.
- **Repeated addition:** Adding the same number many times
- **Multiplicand:** The number to be multiplied
- **Multiplier:** The number which determines the number of times the multiplicand is to be multiplied
- **Product:** The result of multiplication of two numbers
- Multiplication with 0 gives 0 always.
- Multiplication with 1 gives the number itself.
- To **double** a number, multiply the number by 2 or add the number to itself.
- Numbers can be multiplied horizontally as well as vertically.
- We learnt,
  - Multiplication of 2- and 3-digit numbers with 1-digit numbers without regrouping
  - Multiplication of 2-digit numbers with 1-digit numbers with regrouping
- **Word problems on multiplication:** Getting familiar with real-life applications of multiplication

Chapter Revision

A. Complete the table.

	Multiplication Statement	Multiplier	Multiplicand	Product
1.	6 × 7	______	______	______
2.	0 × 10	______	______	______
3.	1 × 9	______	______	______
4.	5 × 5	______	______	______

B. Choose the correct option.

1. 2 × 5
   a. 11 b. 12 c. 10 d. 25
2. 10 × 4
   a. 40 b. 14 c. 10 d. 4
3. 7 × 7
   a. 17 b. 49 c. 70 d. 7
4. 6 × 90
   a. 45 b. 54 c. 16 d. 540

C. Fill the missing terms using multiplication tables.

1. 4, ____, ____, 16, ____
2. 7, ____, 21, ____, 35
3. 3, ____, ____, 12, 15
4. 9, 18, ____, ____, ____

D. Fill in the blanks.

1. 4 times 6 is ______
2. The products in the table of 2 end with ______, ______, ______, ______ or 8.
3. The products in the table of 5 end with ______ and ______ alternatively.
4. The products in the table of 10 end with ______.

E. Find the product.

1. 30 × 2 = ______
2. 40 × 5 = ______
3. 4 × 2 = ______
4. 5 × 3 = ______
5. 8 × 5 = ______
6. 9 × 1 = ______
7. 4 × 0 = ______
8. 6 × 10 = ______

F. Solve the following word problems.

1. Dhruv eats 4 sandwiches every day. How many sandwiches can he eat in 8 days?
2. A lunch box costs ₹120. How much will be the cost of 3 lunch boxes?
3. If 5 people can sit in one car, how many people can sit in 16 cars?

SKILL UP!

A. 21 CS Critical Thinking, Information Literacy

Count the number of students in your class. Write a multiplication statement for the total number of students. Can you write more than one multiplication statement?

B. Count the number of family members in your best friend's family. Add that number to the number of family members in your family. Now, write the multiplication statements for the total number of family members.

C. 21 CS Critical Thinking, Information Literacy HQ Living In An Interconnected Society

1 NO POVERTY

Madhu's mother wants to give stationery items to school children whose parents could not afford to buy them. The school teacher told her that they needed the items as given in the table.

Help Madhu's mother to find out the exact amount of money needed.

Do you think Madhu's mother is kind-hearted? Have you helped anyone in any way? Specify.

Stationery items	Quantity	Cost of 1 item (₹)	Total cost
Notebook	9	20	9×20
Pencil	8	3	8×3
Eraser	7	4	7×4
Sharpener	6	5	6×5
Pencil box	5	10	5×10

SUSTAINABLE DEVELOPMENT GOALS

Question C is in line with SDG 1 No Poverty. There are many children in our country who can not afford to buy books and stationery items due to poverty. A pencil box is a luxury for some, but not all can afford it. Children missing school due to poverty would prevent them from getting a quality education (SDG 4). So, what do you think you can do to help those children who can not buy pencils or go to school?

WORKSHEET 7

21 CS Life Skills HQ Harmony In The Self

15 LIFE ON LAND

Karan and Veda are throwing trash bags in the dustbin.

1. If Karan and Veda throw 2 trash bags each, there will be 2 × 2 ______ trash bags in the dustbin.
2. If their fathers join them and throw the same number of trash bags as they are, there will be 4 × 2 = ______ trash bags in the dustbin.
3. Should we throw the garbage on the roads or in the river? Why or why not?

____

We should always carry our garbage and throw it in a dustbin!

8 Division

Learning Objectives

- To understand division as equal sharing, equal grouping and repeated subtraction
- To learn division on the number line
- To understand the terms used in division
- To understand the properties of division

Let's Get Started

21 CS Critical Thinking HQ Understanding Values In Relationships

Ankit has 6 balloons. He wants to distribute these balloons equally among him and his two friends.

Look at the picture given below. Has Amit distributed the balloons equally among him and his friends? __________

Each child should get _______ balloons.

DIVISION AS EQUAL SHARING

Division can be explained as equal sharing. Share 8 toffees among 4 boys such that each boy gets the same number of toffees.

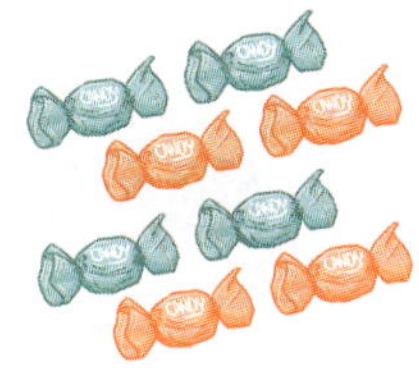

We find that when we share 8 toffees equally among 4 boys, then each boy gets 2 toffees and there are no toffees left.

This can be explained by the following division statement.

NOTE

÷ is the symbol of division.

8	÷	4	=	2
↓		↓		↓
Total number of toffees		Number of boys		Number of toffees each boy got

Example 1: Share 9 bananas equally among 3 monkeys.

9 bananas

9 ÷ 3 = 3. Each monkey gets 3 bananas.

DIVISION AS EQUAL GROUPING

Division can also be explained as equal grouping.

Put 10 pencils in equal groups of 2 each.

We find that when we make groups of 2 each out of 10 pencils, we get 5 groups.

This can be explained by the following division statement.

10 ÷ 2 = **5**

Example 2: Put 12 stars in equal groups of 6 each.

How many groups do you get? 12 ÷ 6 = ☐

EXERCISE 8A

1. Share 12 apples equally among 4 children.

Each child will get _____ apples.

$12 \div 4 = \square$

2. Share 6 bones equally between 2 dogs.

Each dog will get _____ bones.

$6 \div 2 = \square$

3. Share 12 pieces of cheese equally among 3 mice.

Each mouse will get _____ pieces of cheese.

$12 \div 3 = \square$

4. Put 14 balls in equal groups of 7 each.

How many groups are there that carry 7 balls each?

$14 \div 7 = \square$

5. Put 15 butterflies in equal groups of 5 each.

How many groups are there that carry 5 butterflies each?

$15 \div 5 = \square$

DIVISION AS REPEATED SUBTRACTION

Division can also be explained as repeated subtraction.

Example 3: 12 ÷ 3 = ☐

To get the answer of this question, we subtract 3 from 12 and keep subtracting 3 from the answer till we get 0.

Then, we count the number of times 3 is subtracted. That will be our answer.

12
−3 = 9 (1)
−3 = 6 (2)
−3 = 3 (3)
−3 = 0 (4)

We subtracted 3 **four times** from 12 to reach 0.

So, 12 ÷ 3 = 4

Example 4: 15 ÷ 5 = ☐

15
−5 = 10 (1)
−5 = 5 (2)
−5 = 0 (3)

We subtracted 5 **three times** from 15 to reach 0.

So, 15 ÷ 5 = 3

DIVISION USING NUMBER LINE

Division can also be explained on the number line.

Number line is a line on which numbers are arranged in an order.

Example 5: Show 6 ÷ 2 on the number line.

Solution: Start from 6 and jump 2 numbers every time till you reach 0. How many times did you jump?

MENTAL MATHS

Find out the answers through repeated subtraction.

1. 15 ÷ 3
2. 18 ÷ 9
3. 30 ÷ 10

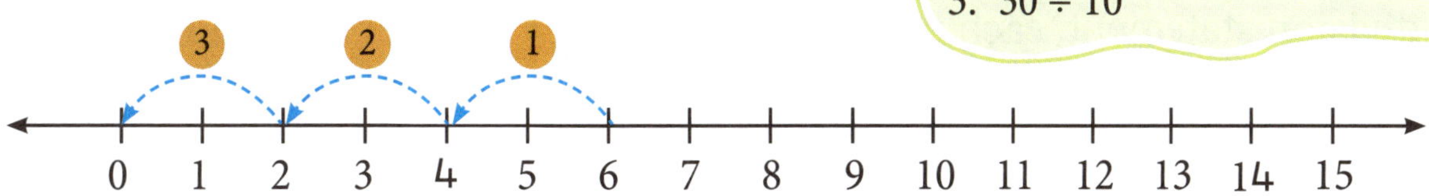

As you jumped 3 times to reach 0, the answer is 3. That is, 6 ÷ 2 = **3**

Example 6: Show 12 ÷ 3 on the number line.

Solution:

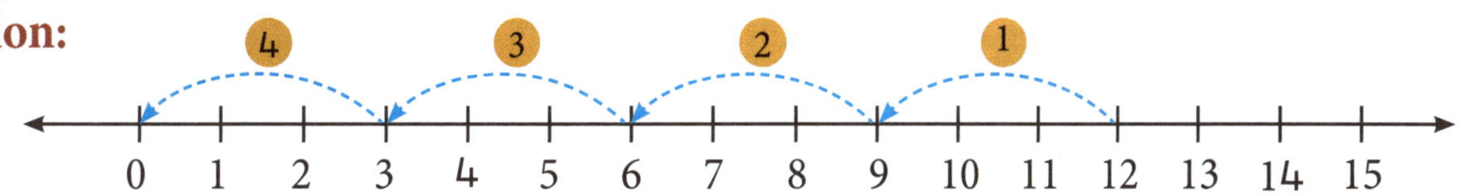

As there are 4 jumps from 12 to 0, the answer is 4. That is, 12 ÷ 3 = 4

EXERCISE 8B

1. **Solve the following using repeated subtraction. Write the division statements.**

   a. 50 ÷ 5 = _____ b. 48 ÷ 8 = _____ c. 63 ÷ 9 = _____ d. 16 ÷ 4 = _____

2. **Write the division statements for the following.**

   a.

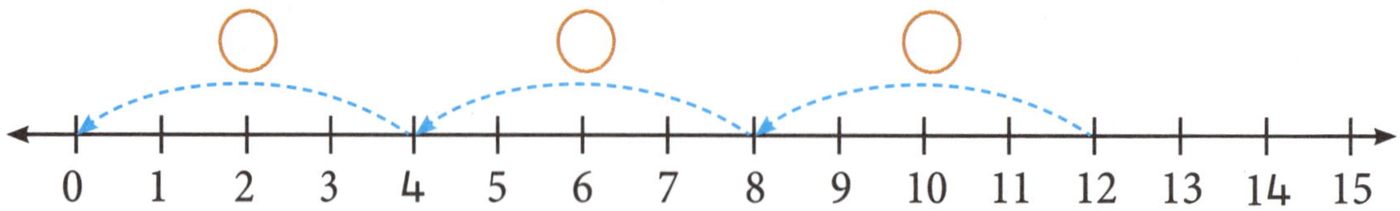

   b.

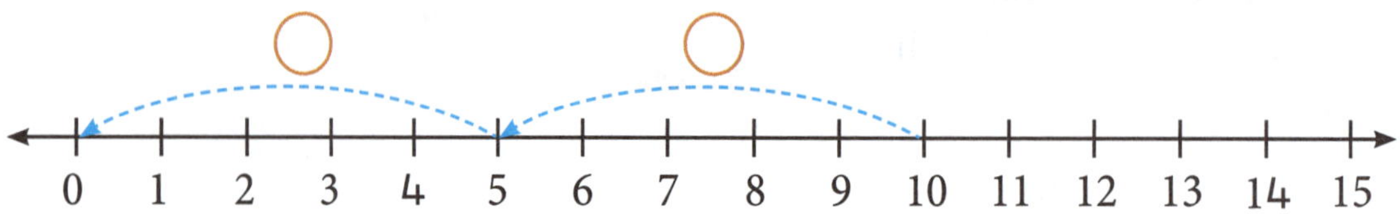

3. **Solve using number line.**

   a. 12 ÷ 2 = _____

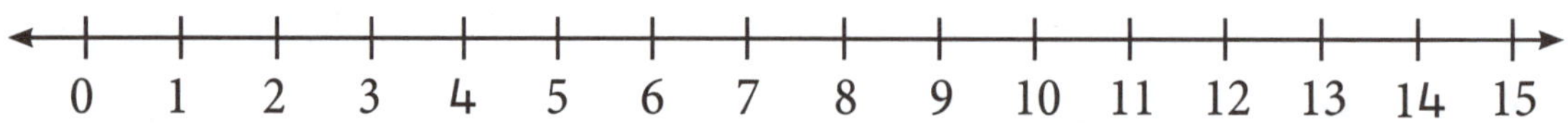

   b. 15 ÷ 3 = _____

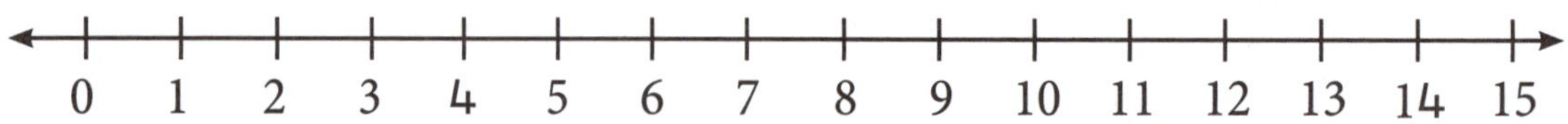

TERMS USED IN DIVISION

In a division statement, each number has a name. Consider the following division statement.

10 ÷ 2 = **5**

> 10 is the dividend.
> 2 is the divisor.
> 5 is the quotient.

Dividend is the number which is being divided.

Divisor is the number which divides the dividend.

Quotient is the result of the division statement.

PROPERTIES OF DIVISION

1. **Dividing a number by 1 is always equal to the number itself.**

Example: Share 5 chocolates with 1 child.

$5 \div 1 = \mathbf{5}$

5 chocolates

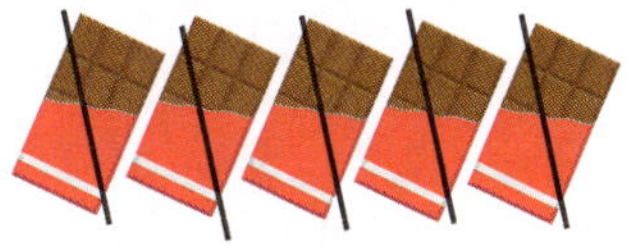

1 child gets all the 5 chocolates.

2. **Dividing a number by itself is always equal to 1.**

Example: Share 5 chocolates equally among 5 children.

5 chocolates

$5 \div 5 = \mathbf{1}$

1 child gets 1 chocolate.

3. **Dividing zero by a number is always equal to 0.**

Example: Share 0 chocolates equally among 5 children.
Since there are zero chocolates, each child gets 0 chocolates.

$0 \div 5 = \mathbf{0}$

4. **Dividing a number by zero is not possible.**

Example: Share 5 chocolates equally among zero children.

Since there are no children, it is not possible to do this division.

$5 \div 0 =$ Not possible

GO EASY!

If you remember the multiplication tables well, then division will become easier.

MENTAL MATHS

1. $25 \div 1 =$ ______
2. $17 \div 17 =$ ______
3. $0 \div 19 =$ ______

NOTE

There is a relationship between multiplication and division. Multiplication is the opposite of division. Division is the opposite of multiplication.
If $4 \times 2 = 8$, then $8 \div 4 = 2$ and $8 \div 2 = 4$.

COMMON ERRORS

$\frac{0}{5} = 5$ ✗ $\frac{0}{5} = 0$ ✓

$\frac{9}{0} = 0$ ✗ $\frac{9}{0} =$ Not Possible ✓

MATHS LAB ACTIVITY

21 CS Technology Literacy, Life Skills EL

Aim: To reinforce the concept of division as equal grouping

Materials required: 15 marbles, 3 bowls

Procedure:

1. Take 15 marbles and 3 empty bowls.
2. Put one marble at a time in the 3 bowls till all the 15 marbles are put in them.
3. How many marbles do you manage to put in each bowl?

   15 marbles in 3 bowls can be placed one by one, as shown.

   This can be written as 15 ÷ 3 = 5.

   That is, 5 marbles are placed in each bowl.

Conclusion: Equal grouping means to make groups of items in such a way that each group has an equal number of items.

CONCEPT MAP

Division

- Division as equal sharing
- Division as equal grouping
- Division as repeated subtraction
- Division using number line
- Properties of division

KEY CONCEPTS

- **Division:** A method to share or group equally
- **Equal sharing:** To distribute something in a way that it is shared equally
- **Equal grouping:** To make groups of items in such a way that each group has an equal number of items
- **Repeated subtraction:** It is another way to understand division, where we subtract the same number many times from the total, till we get zero.
- **Number line:** A line in which the numbers are given in an order
- **Dividend** is the number which is being divided. **Divisor** is the number which divides the dividend. **Quotient** is the result of division statement.
- Division by 1 is equal to the number itself. Division by the number itself gives 1. Dividing 0 by a number gives 0. Dividing a number by 0 is not possible.

Chapter Revision

A. Fill in the blanks.

1. 6 ÷ 2 = _____ 
2. 8 ÷ 4 = _____ 
3. 10 ÷ 2 = _____ 
4. 12 ÷ 3 = _____ 
5. If 5 × 2 = 10, then 10 ÷ 5 = _____ and 10 ÷ 2 = _____

B. Write T for true and F for false.

1. 21 ÷ 7 as repeated subtraction is 3. [ ]

```
 21
 -7  —
 ----
 14
 -7  —
 ----
  7
 -7  —
 ----
  0
```

2. 16 ÷ 8 as repeated subtraction is 2. [ ]

```
 16
 -8  —
 ----
  8
 -8  —
 ----
  0
```

3. a. 14 ÷ 7 on the number line is 4. [ ]

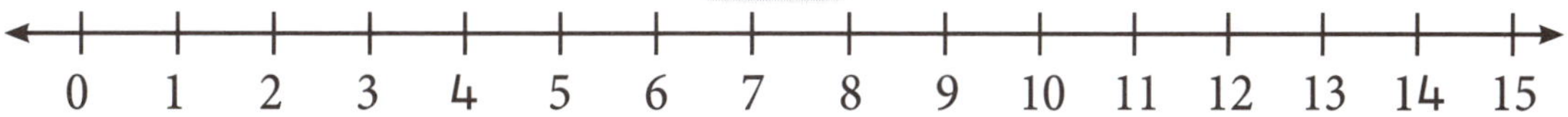

b. 10 ÷ 5 on the number line is 2. [ ]

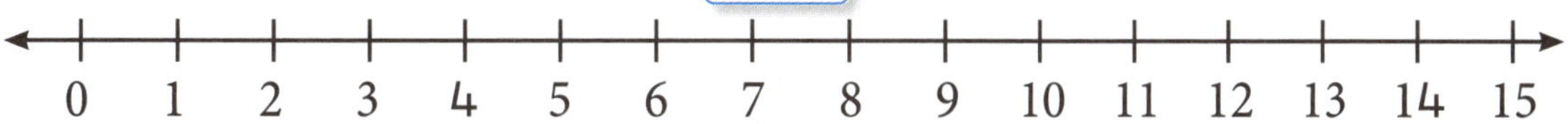

4. 8 ÷ 8 = 8 [ ]
5. 0 ÷ 9 = 0 [ ]
6. 10 ÷ 0 = 10 [ ]

C. Solve the following word problems.

1. Aman wanted to colour 6 pages equally in 3 days. How many pages should he colour every day?

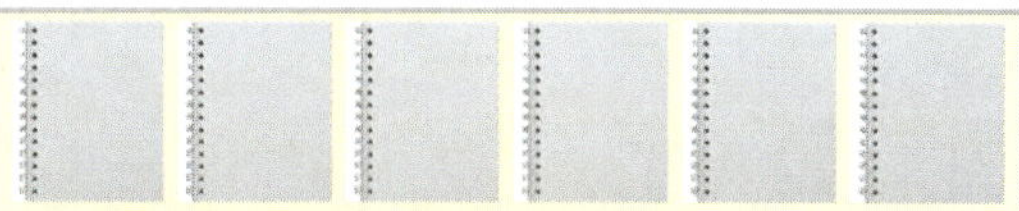

He should colour _____ pages every day.

2. Tarana wants to eat 10 apples equally in 5 days. How many apples should she eat every day?

She should eat _____ apples every day.

3. There are 35 packets of refreshments for a group of 5 friends. Find out how many packets each friend can get, if distributed equally.

SKILL UP!

A. 21 CS Collaboration EL

Try making the following equal groups of students in your class. How many groups do you make?

1. Take 6 students and make groups of 2 students each.

   Number of groups = ________________

   Therefore, 6 ÷ 2 = ________________

2. Take 16 students and make groups of 4 students each.

   Number of groups = ________________

   Therefore, 16 ÷ 4 = ________________

B. 21 CS Life Skills HQ Harmony In The Self

While playing a game, the teacher needed groups of 2 students each. There were 7 students. How many groups will be made?

We can make __________ groups and 1 child is left alone.

Should we add one more child to make another group or should we let the seventh child be alone?

C. 21 CS Critical Thinking

If we arrange 9 marbles in groups of 2, how many groups do we get?

1. We get ________ groups and ________ extra marble.
2. If we want 5 groups, how many more marbles do we need? ________
3. If we want 6 groups, how many more marbles do we need? ________

SUSTAINABLE DEVELOPMENT GOALS

Question B is in line with SDG 10 Reduced Inequalities. We should never let anyone feel left out! Be thoughtful about others from a young age. Understand that everyone is equal and everyone should get equal opportunities. You can reduce inequality this way.

WORKSHEET 8

21 CS Critical Thinking HQ Happiness My Goal

Meena is making five goody bags to give as return gifts on her birthday party. Help her to find out how many of each item she can put in one goody bag. Should Meena put equal quantities of items in each bag?

In each bag, she can put

1. __________ toffees
2. __________ sharpener
3. __________ stars
4. __________ chocolate
5. __________ crayon box

Why Meena is focusing on equal sharing? Any specific reason for that?

9 Measurement

Learning Objectives

- To express and measure length in metres and centimetres
- To express and measure mass in kilograms and grams
- To express and measure capacity in litres and millilitres

Let's Get Started

21 CS Information Literacy

CC Integration with Environmental Studies

1. Fill in the blanks using the correct option.
   a. The elephant is _________ than the zebra. (bigger/smaller)
   b. The monkey is _________ than the giraffe. (taller/shorter)
   c. The zebra is _________ than the monkey. (heavier/lighter)

2. The length of this pen = _________ paper clips.

3. If the water of this jug is poured out, can it fill 3 glasses or 3 buckets? _________ (3 glasses/3 buckets)

MEASURING LENGTH

We learnt about some non-standard units of length in Class 1 such as handspan, footspan, cubit or pace. These non-standard units give different measurements of the same objects. How do we get exact measurements?

Metre and Centimetre

To have an exact measurement of length instead of an estimation, the standard units of measurement are used.

These are '**metre**' and '**centimetre**'.

We have a fixed tool to measure the length of any short object, like a ruler.

> **NOTE**
>
> Relationship between metre and centimetre
>
> **1 m = 100 cm**

A **metre** is used to measure longer lengths. It is approximately equal to the distance between both your hands, if you stretch them. A metre is written as **m** in short form.

When you buy a piece of cloth, the shopkeeper measures it in metres.

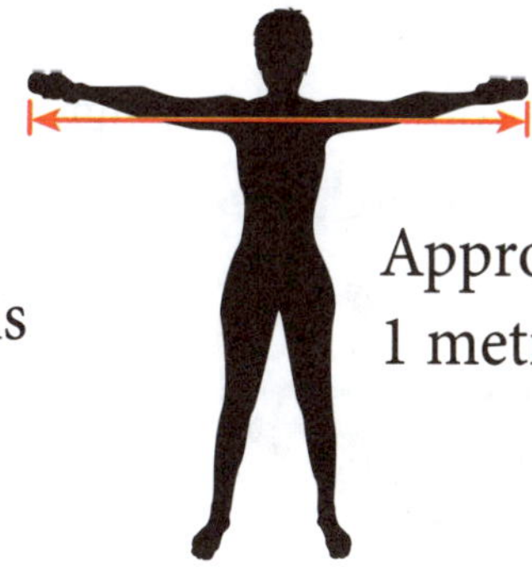

Approximately 1 metre

A **centimetre** is used to measure shorter lengths. It is written as **cm** in its short form.

Look at the ruler to see the length of a centimetre.

This length is equal to 1 cm.

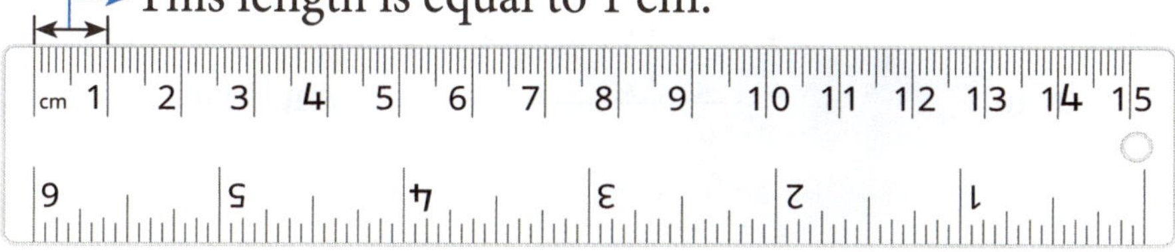

Let us measure the length of a few objects using a ruler.

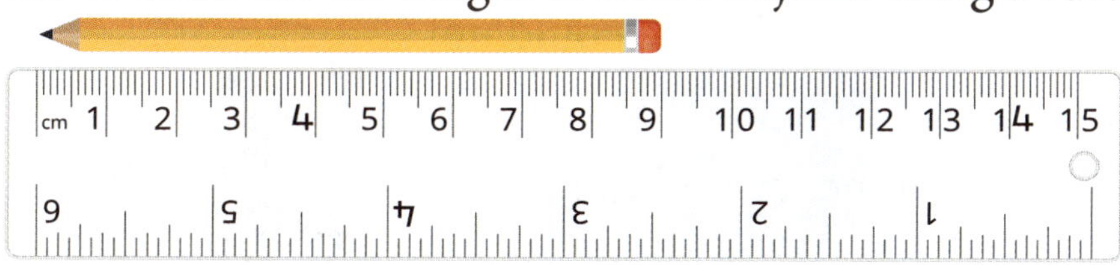

The length of the pencil is 9 cm.

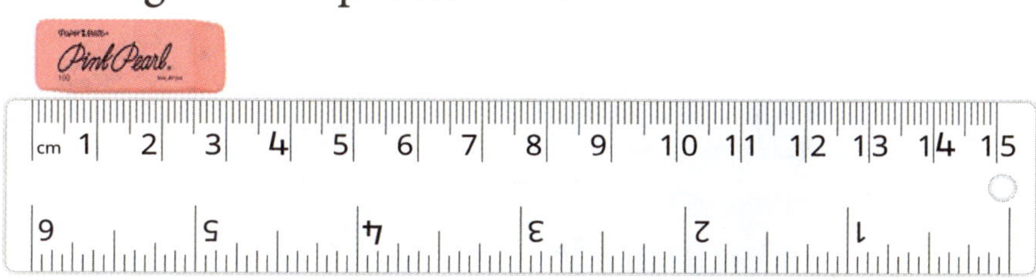

What is the length of this eraser? ☐ cm

> **GO EASY!**
>
> To measure the length of an object with a ruler, place the one end of the object at 0 cm mark of the ruler and note the measure on the ruler at another end of the object.

EXERCISE 9A

1. Which is a longer measurement—metre or centimetre? ____________
2. Circle the pictures which you think are less than 1 metre.

a. Length of a train

b. Length of a pencil box

c. Height of a door

d. Length of a wallet

3. Circle the pictures which you think are more than 1 centimetre.

a. dot

b. Length of a pen

c. Length of a sharpener

d. Length of a shoe

4. Write which measurement (m or cm) can be used to measure the following.

a. Length of a bed ____________

b. Length of a thumb ____________

c. Length of a wall ____________

d. Height of a big cupboard ____________

MEASURING MASS

Arijit could carry his school bag on his back, but he could not pick up a large suitcase.

That is because the large suitcase is too heavy and the school bag is lighter in mass.

Weigh less than the glass

Weigh more than the glass

Try picking up various objects to see which is heavier and which is lighter.

Kilograms and Grams

Simple balance

We can measure the mass of an object using some non-standard units like stones, marbles, etc.

A simple balance or weighing balance is used to weigh things.

We use standard units like '**kilogram**' and '**gram**' to weigh objects.

Kilogram is written as '**kg**' in short form.

Gram is written as '**g**' in short form.

Kilogram is used to weigh heavier objects and gram is used to weigh lighter objects.

> **NOTE**
>
> Relationship between gram and kilogram
>
> **1 kg = 1000 g**

A teaspoon of salt weighs about 5 g.
A tablespoon of salt weighs about 15 g.

2 big pieces of ginger weigh about 100 g.
5 big pieces of ginger weigh about 250 g.

3 apples weigh about 500 g.
6 apples weigh about 1 kg.

> **MENTAL MATHS**
>
> Look for an object less than 15 cm around you.
> Look for an object heavier than your pencil around you.

EXERCISE 9B

1. How much would each object weigh? Circle the correct option.

a. 

2 kg or 2 g

b. 

10 kg or 10 g

c. 

5 kg or 5 g

d. 

100 kg or 100 g

2. Circle the objects which you think can weigh more than 1 kg.

3. Write how much each of the following objects would weigh. Fill in the boxes using: 500 g, 250 g, 1 kg, 100 g. (*Hint*: Check the size of weights.)

a.

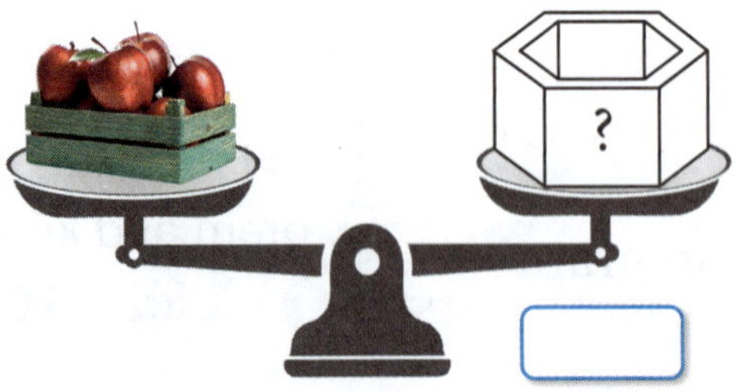

b.

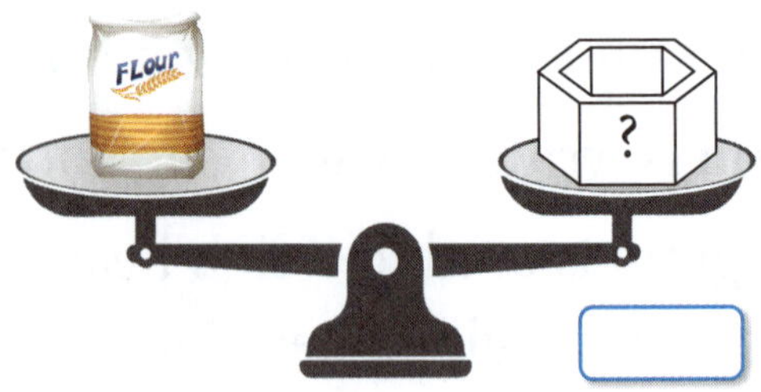

c.

d.

MEASURING CAPACITY

We know that the capacity of a container is equal to the amount of liquid that it can hold.

We can measure the capacities of containers using some non-standard units like cups, spoons, buckets, etc.

How many spoons of sugar will fill the bowl?

If 20 spoons of sugar fill the bowl, then we say that the capacity of the bowl is equal to 20 spoons.

Litres and Millilitres

We use standard units like '**litres**' and '**millilitres**' to measure capacity. **Litres** is written as 'ℓ' and **millilitres** is written as 'mℓ' in short forms.

Millilitre is used to measure smaller quantities of liquid.

Litre is used to measure larger quantities of liquid.

NOTE

Relationship between litre and millilitre

1 ℓ = 1000 mℓ

1 teaspoon of liquid medicine is about 5 mℓ.

1 tablespoon of liquid medicine is about 15 mℓ.

A glass of water is about 200 mℓ.

A bucket of water is about 15 ℓ.

NOTE

Why do we use the word, 'about', in measurement?
It means that the measurement is not exact. It is an estimate.

DO YOU KNOW?

What do you think is the smallest measure of water that you might have seen?
A drop!

EXERCISE 9C

1. Circle the correct measurement.

a. 5 mℓ or 5 ℓ

b. 1 mℓ or 1 ℓ

c. 250 mℓ or 250 ℓ

d. 20 mℓ or 20 ℓ

2. Tick (✓) the objects which can be measured in litres. Cross (×) the objects which can be measured in millilitres.

a.  ☐

b.  ☐

c. 

☐

d. 

☐

e.  ☐

GO EASY!

Remember the units of measuring length, mass and capacity.

Length = m, cm Mass = g, kg Capacity = mℓ, ℓ

Maths Lab Activity

21 CS Technology Literacy EL STEAM CHALLENGE

Aim: To reinforce the concept of capacity

Materials required: A jug and a glass

Procedure: Given that each glass of water measures 200 mℓ.

1. Take one glass of water at a time and pour it in a jug. Do this 5 times.

   200 mℓ + 200 mℓ + 200 mℓ + 200 mℓ + 200 mℓ
2. After the addition, you will find that the jug now contains 1000 mℓ of water.

   5 glasses of water = 1000 mℓ, which is equal to 1 litre.
3. Observe, and by adding more water, check what would be the capacity of the jug.

Concept Map

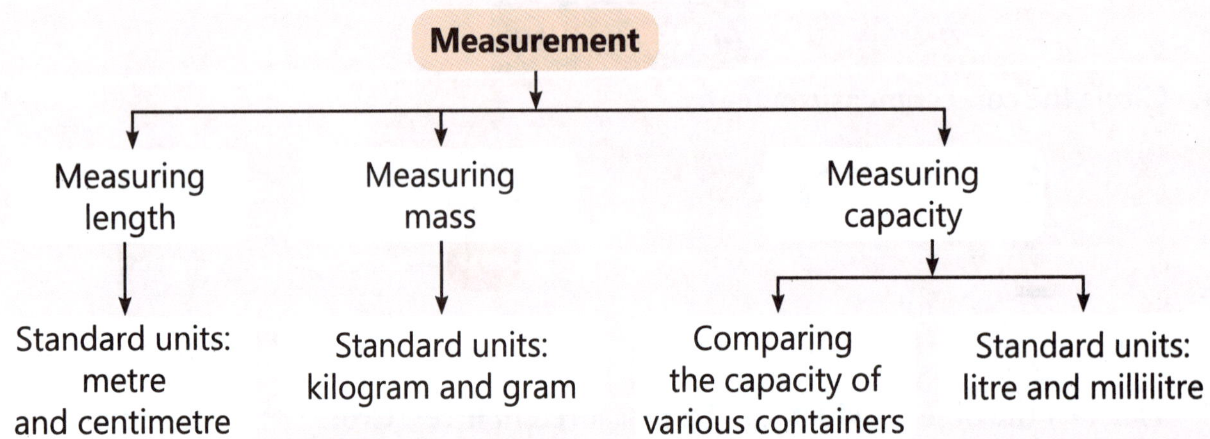

Key Concepts

- The standard units of measuring length are centimetre and metre.
- **Metre:** A unit of length to measure longer objects. Short form is 'm'.
- **Centimetre:** A unit of length to measure shorter objects. Short form is 'cm'.
- The standard units of measuring mass are gram and kilogram.
- **Kilogram:** A unit of mass to measure heavier objects. Short form is 'kg'.
- **Gram:** A unit of mass to measure lighter objects. Short form is 'g'.
- The standard units of measuring capacity are millilitre and litre.
- **Litre:** A unit of capacity to measure larger quantities of liquid. Short form is 'ℓ'.
- **Millilitre:** A unit of capacity to measure smaller quantities of liquid. Short form is 'mℓ'.

A. Tick (✓) the correct length.

1. 

The length of the sofa is about 2 cm/2 m.

2. 

The length of this wallet is about 15 cm/15 m.

B. How much will each of the following weigh? Tick (✓) the correct option.

1. 

The mass of this orange is about 100 g/100 kg.

2. 

Rahul weighs about 15 g/15 kg.

C. Tick (✓) the correct capacity.

1. The amount of eye drops in this bottle is about 20 mℓ/20 ℓ. 

2. The amount of oil in this container is about 5 mℓ/5 ℓ. 

D. Fill in the blanks.

1. The fixed units to measure length are _______ and _______. (ℓ, mℓ/m, cm)
2. The length of a notebook will be measured in _______. (m/cm)
3. Mass is measured in _______ and _______. (m, cm/g, kg)
4. Three onions will weigh in _______. (g, kg)
5. The capacity of a container is measured in _______. (ℓ/m)

E. Choose the correct option.

1. Metre measures a _______ (longer/shorter) length than centimetre.
2. Gram measures a _______ (lighter/heavier) mass than kilogram.
3. Litre measures a _______ (greater/smaller) capacity than millilitre.

SKILL UP!

A. 21 CS Technology Literacy, Life Skills | EL

Pick up a few objects in your house and measure the length of each using a ruler. A few examples are shown below.

1.  = _____ cm
2.  = _____ cm
3.  = _____ cm
4.  = _____ cm

B. 21 CS Critical Thinking, Life Skills | CC Integration with Science | HQ Coexisting with Nature

Aditi filled 8 litres of water in a bucket. She used 6 litres to water the plants in the pots. She threw the rest of the water. How much water did she throw away? Is it okay to waste water?

C. 21 CS Critical Thinking | EL | STEAM CHALLENGE

Fill a bucket with a mug and a jug. 12 jugs of water can fill the bucket. If we try to fill the bucket with mugs, will it be more than 12 or less than 12 jugs? Why?

SUSTAINABLE DEVELOPMENT GOALS

Question B is in line with SDG 15 Life on Land. Plants are important to us. They make the Earth green and provide us with food. Find out other uses of plants. After finding the answer to this, you will understand why we need more plants and why SDG 15 is important. Find out why wasting water is not good, and which SDG talks about water.

WORKSHEET 9

21 CS Critical Thinking, Information Literacy | CC Integration with Physical Education | HQ Knowing My Needs | 3 GOOD HEALTH AND WELL-BEING

Sachin, Saif and Anuj were running in a race. Observe the picture and answer the following.

In 3 minutes, Sachin ran 395 metres. He drank 4 glasses of water after the race.

In 3 minutes, Saif ran 409 metres. He drank 1 glass of water after the race.

In 3 minutes, Anuj ran 389 metres. He drank 3 glasses of water after the race.

1. Which child came first in the race? How many metres did he run in 3 minutes?

   ____

2. Which child drank the maximum glasses of water? How many glasses of water did he drink?

   ____

3. Arrange the names of the children in the ascending order of the metres covered by them in the race.

   ____

4. Tick (✓) the correct unit of measurement.

   a. Weight of a child

      g, kg

   b. Amount of water in one glass

      mℓ, ℓ

Should we exercise regularly? ________

It is very good for our health!

We must spend some time everyday to play outdoor games and exercise.

10 Shapes and Patterns

Learning Objectives

- To learn about the different types of lines
- To understand what are corners and edges
- To identify flat and solid shapes
- To identify rolling and sliding objects
- To recognise different patterns based on their shapes, numbers and letters

Let's Get Started

21 CS Information Literacy AI

1. Colour the given shapes according to their colour codes.

Colour codes

- Blue
- Yellow
- Green
- Red

2. Match the shapes in Column A to their names in Column B.

Column A	Column B
	Triangle
	Square
	Rectangle
	Circle

LINES

A line is a long mark that extends in both directions without any end. Lines can be straight or curved.

> **Go Easy!**
>
> The word 'Horizontal' starts with the letter H, which has a line —— in the middle. This helps us to learn that horizontal lines move from left to right like ——.
>
> The word 'Curve' starts with the letter C, which itself is a curve.

Straight Lines

Straight lines move straight in both directions. They can be **vertical, horizontal** or **slanting**.

Vertical lines	Horizontal lines	Slanting lines
Also called standing lines.	Also called sleeping lines.	Also called oblique lines.
They run straight up and down the page.	They run from one side to other side across the page.	They do not go straight across or straight up. They look like a slope and go both up and down and across too.
Electric poles placed on the roads are vertical lines.	The lines on which you write in your notebook are horizontal lines.	The rays of the sun are slanting lines.
Examples: 	**Examples:** 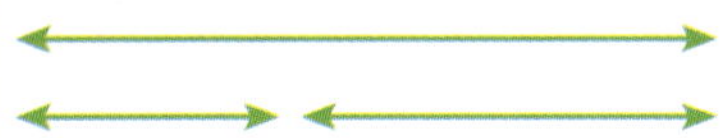	**Examples:** 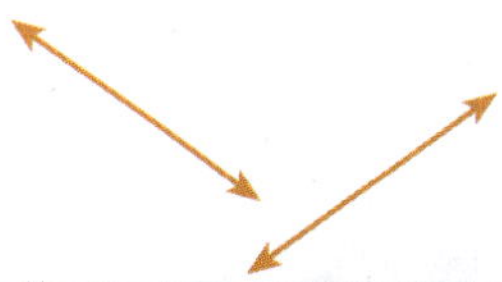

Curved Lines

If a line does not move straight and it bends, then it becomes a **curved** line.

Examples:

A curved road looks like this.

Exercise 10A

Identify and mark the lines as V for vertical, H for horizontal, S for slanting and C for curved.

WHAT ARE CORNERS AND EDGES?

Let us look at the following shapes.

All these shapes are made up of curved or straight lines. These lines are called **sides** or **edges**.

Shapes with straight lines/edges	Shapes with curved lines/edges
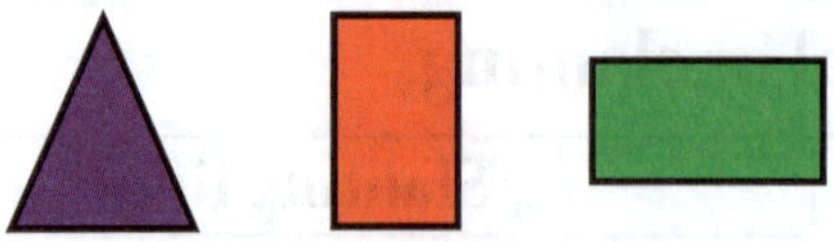	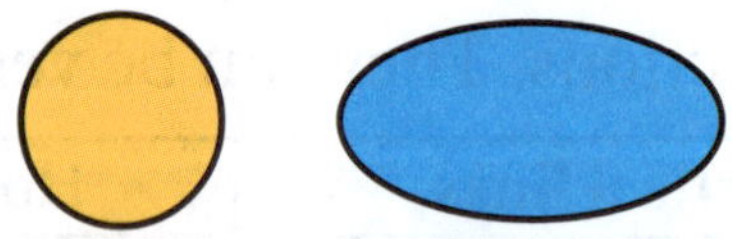

Corners are the points where two sides meet.

FLAT SHAPES

Flat shapes are also called plane shapes.

They can be made from lines or curves.

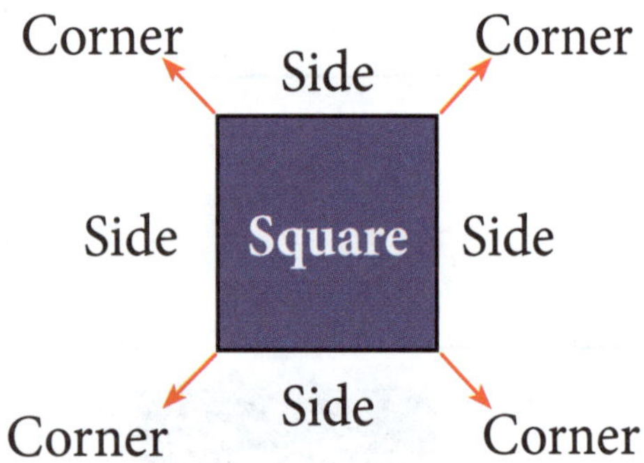

A square has 4 **sides** and 4 **corners**.

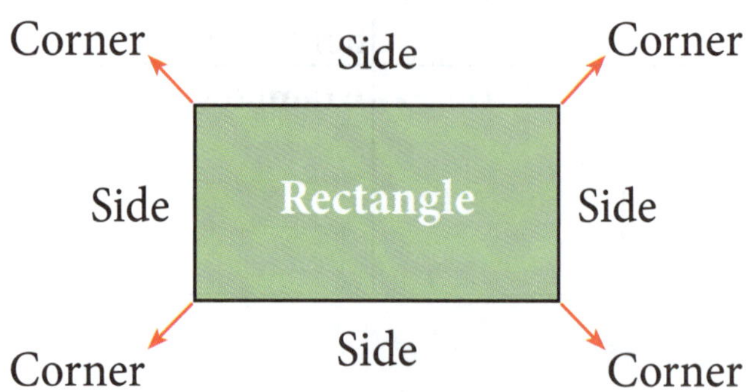

A rectangle has 4 **sides** and 4 **corners**.

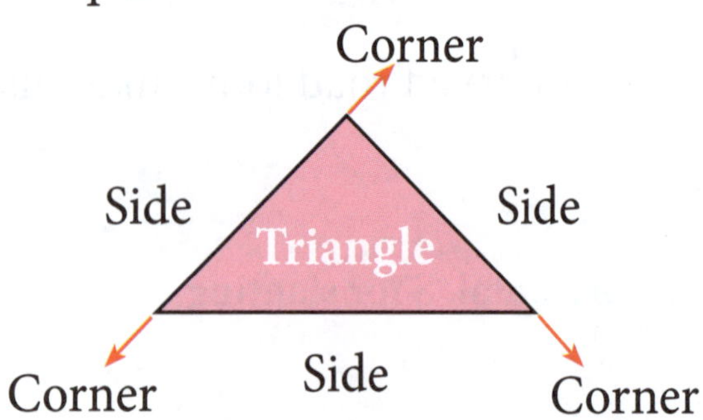

A triangle has **3 sides** and **3 corners**.

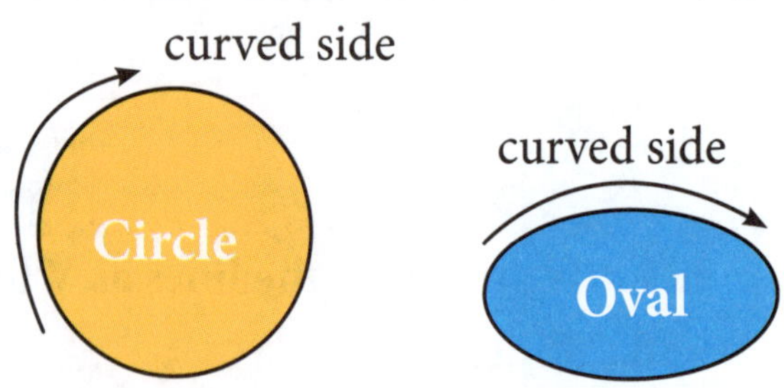

A circle and an oval are made up of a curve. There are **no straight lines or edges.** There are **no corners** in a circle or an oval. They have 1 curved side or curved edge.

DO YOU KNOW?

TRI means 3. That is why a triangle has 3 sides.

Example: A tricycle has 3 wheels.

Flat shapes can also be of different sizes as shown below.

These are squares of different sizes.

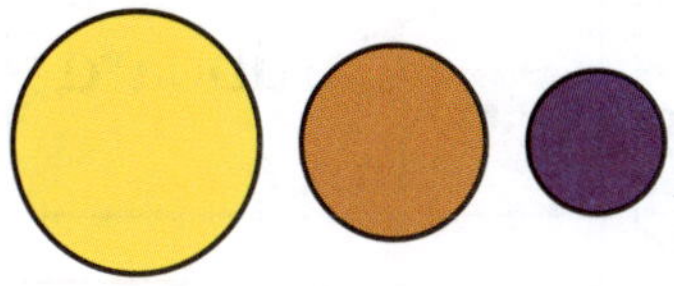

These are circles of different sizes.

Do you know?

The sun looks like a yellow circle.

Exercise 10B

1. Circle the shapes that have 4 corners and 4 sides.

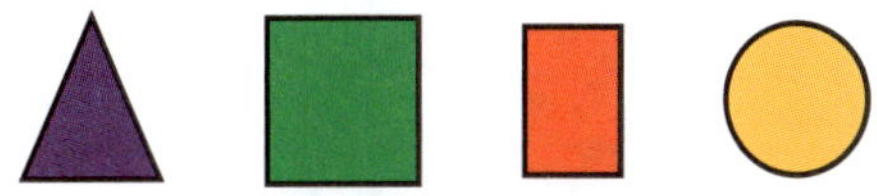

2. Circle the shapes that have no corners.

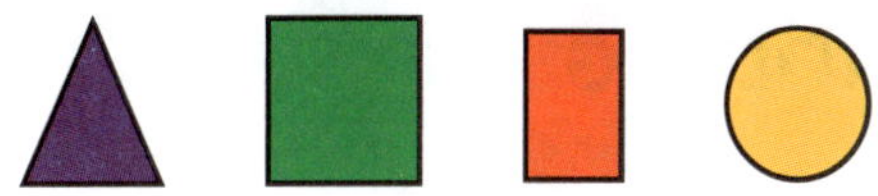

3. Tick (✓) the shapes that are similar to the given coloured shape. Also, cross (×) the shape that is the same size as the coloured shape given.

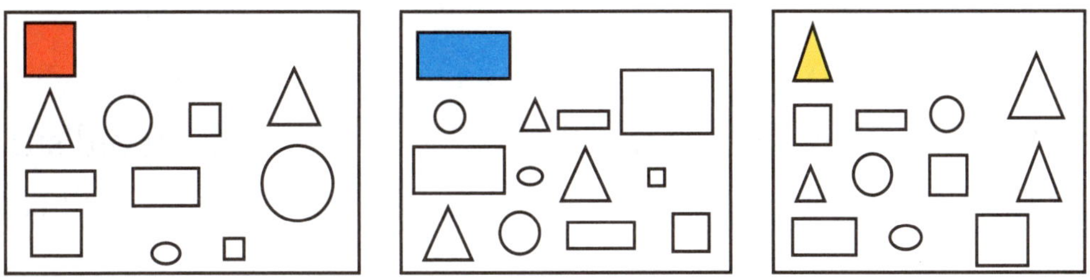

SOLID SHAPES

Solid shapes have length, width and height. Most of the different shapes we see around us are solid shapes. Let us learn about some solid shapes.

CUBE	CUBOID	CYLINDER	SPHERE	CONE
	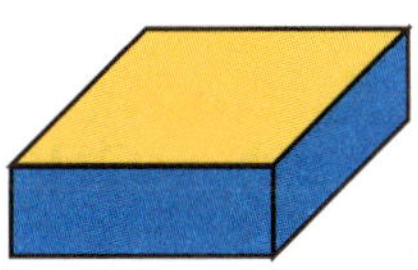	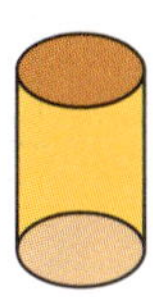	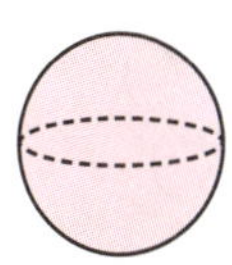	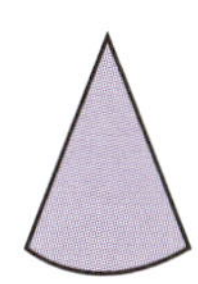
Examples:				

Die	Gift box	Tin can	Basketball	Party cap

SOLID SHAPES AROUND US

When we look around us, we can identify many objects which resemble some of the solid shapes. Let us take a look.

 Cuboid	Cardboard box; Refrigerator
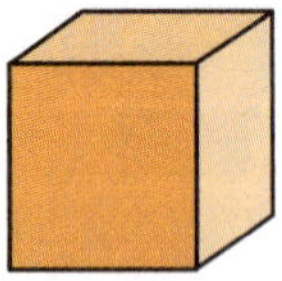 Cube	Tissue box; Ice cube

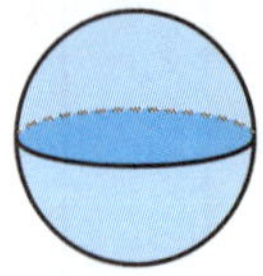 Sphere	Globe; Orange
 Cylinder	Gas cylinder; Water bottle

ROLLING AND SLIDING OBJECTS

When a flat object is pushed, it slides. So, objects that have flat surfaces can slide.

When a curved object is pushed, it rolls. So, objects that have curved surfaces can roll.

Objects that have both flat and curved surfaces can slide as well as roll.

EXERCISE 10C

1. Colour the pictures as per the given instructions.

Colour the
Cuboids – Pink
Cubes – Blue
Spheres – Red
Cones – Purple
Cylinders – Green

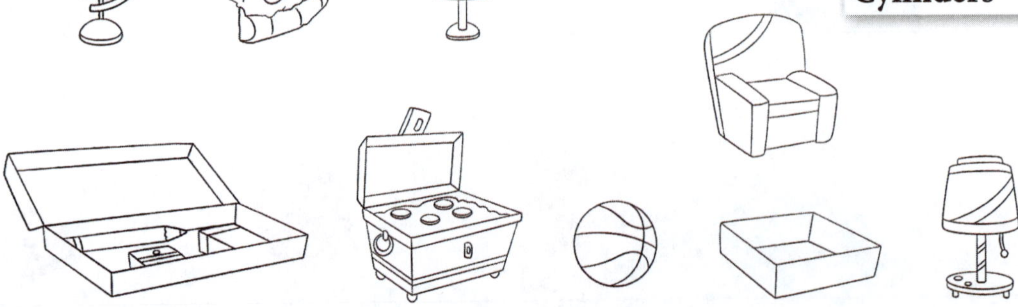

2. **Look at the following objects that you use or see at home and in school. Write down their names in the correct category.**

Food packet | Cell | Eraser | Tissue roll | Water bubbles | Balloon

Cuboid	Cylinder	Sphere
______	______	______
______	______	______

3. **Write R for the objects that roll, S for the objects that slide and RS for the objects that can roll as well as slide.**

a. b. c. d. e. f. g. h. i.

PATTERNS

Pattern is a repeated arrangement of shapes, numbers or letters. If the set of numbers are related to each other in a certain rule or order, then it forms a pattern. Patterns help us to make beautiful decorations.

Examples:

Patterns in shapes

Patterns in letters and numbers

AB	BA	AB	BA	AB	BA
1	2	1	2	1	2

You can make patterns with your handprints and footprints too.

Patterns in Numbers

Observe the number patterns.

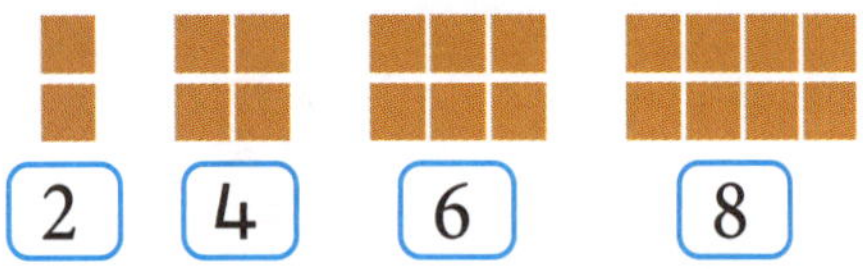

Rule: The number 2 is added each time.

Rule: The number 1 is subtracted each time.

Exercise 10D

Complete the following patterns.

1.  ______

2.  ______

3. 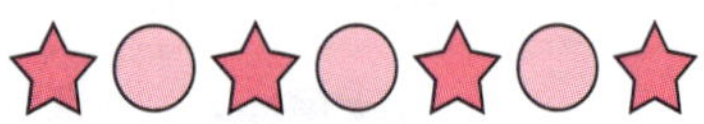 ______

4. 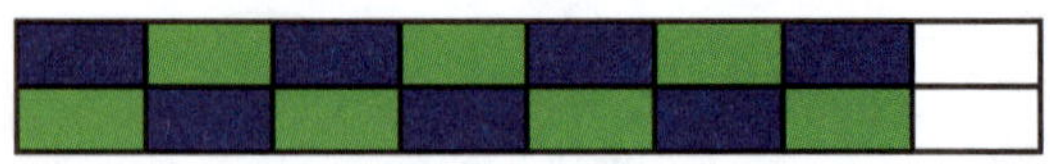

5. 
   4
   ______
   ______
   ______

6. 6, 8, 10, 12, ____, ____, ____ **Rule:** The number ___ is added each time.

PUZZLE!

How will you colour the grid given here with 4 colours of your choice to make a pattern.

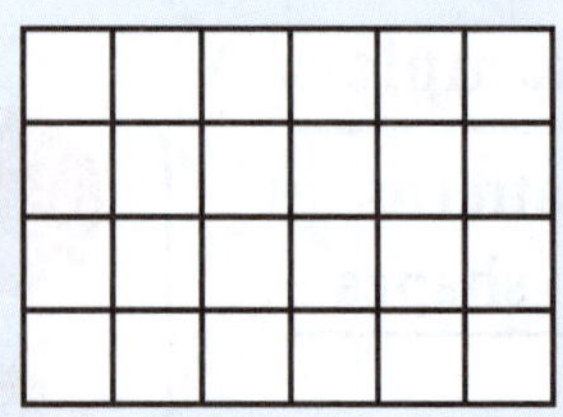

Mental Maths

1. The surface of a
   a. cube is a ______ b. cuboid is a ______ c. cylinder is a ______ d. cone is a ______
2. In a square, the number of sides = ______
3. In a triangle, the number of sides = ______ number of corners = ______
4. In a rectangle, the number of sides = ______ number of corners = ______
5. Which plane shape has no straight sides and no corners? ______

MATHS LAB ACTIVITY

21 CS Critical Thinking, Creativity and Innovation · EL · AI

Aim: To make patterns from things around us

Materials required: Chart paper, colourful buttons, ribbons and some fruits and vegetables

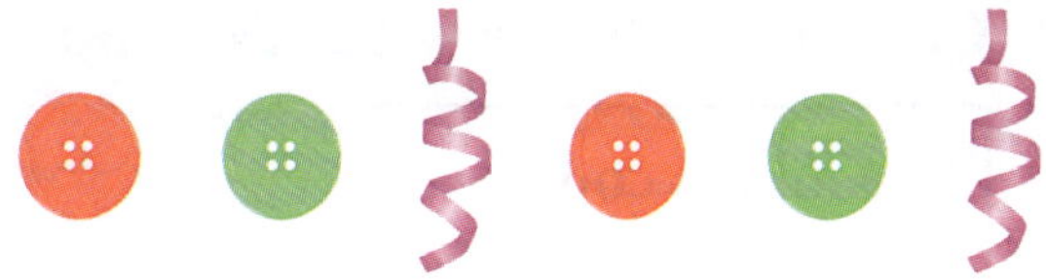

Procedure:

1. On a chart paper, stick a red button, then a green button and then a purple ribbon.
2. Repeat this pattern.
3. Similarly, make patterns using fruits and vegetables like potatoes, onions, oranges and apples.

CONCEPT MAP

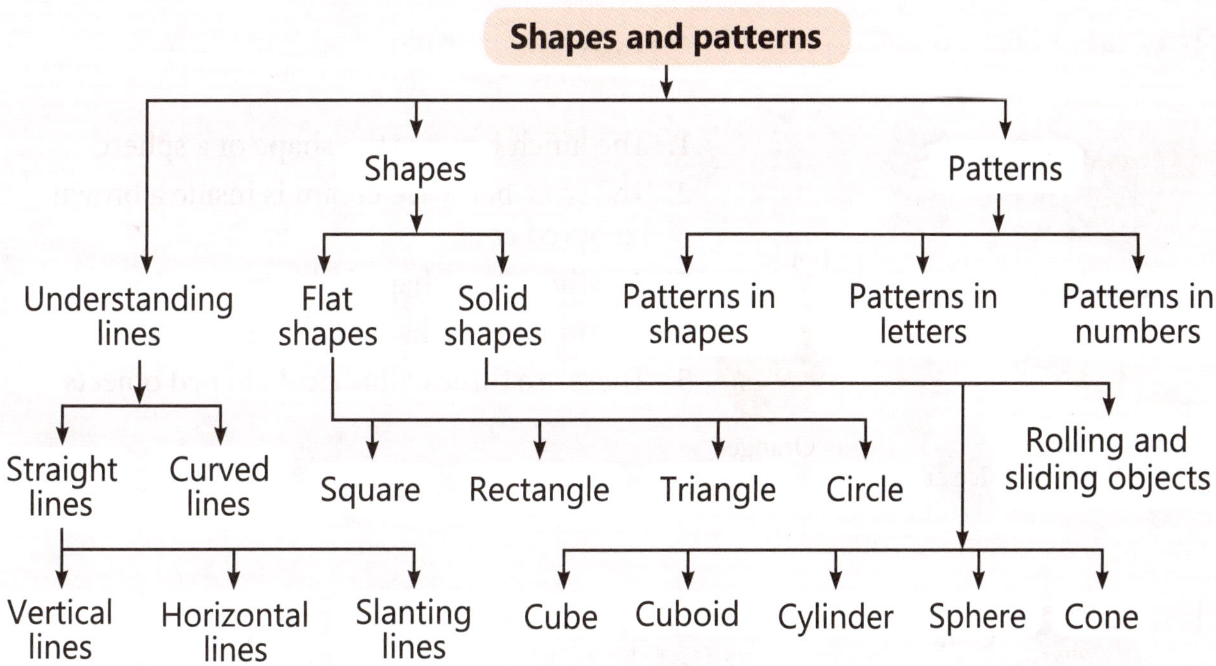

KEY CONCEPTS

- **Lines and curves:** Lines follow a straight path in a certain direction. Curves bend and do not follow a straight path.
- Shapes are made up of straight or curved lines.
- **Corners** are the points where two sides meet.
- Square and rectangle have 4 sides and 4 corners. A triangle has 3 sides and 3 corners. A circle has no straight edges and no corners. It has one curved edge.
- **Flat shapes:** Flat shapes do not have height. They are also called plane shapes.
- **Solid shapes:** Solid shapes have length, width and height.
- **Rolling and sliding objects:** Objects that can roll or slide or both.
- **Patterns** exist in things around us; in shapes, numbers, colours, letters, etc.

Chapter Revision

A. Colour the shapes as per the colour codes.

Colour codes
Square
Rectangle
Triangle
Circle

Look at the red arrows marked here. Write:

V for vertical lines.

H for horizontal lines.

S for slanting lines.

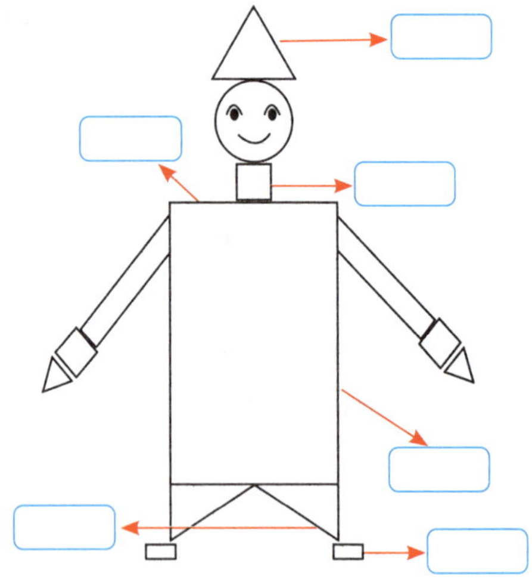

B. These are items from Ms Neera's kitchen. Write T for true and F for false.

Microwave

Lunch box

Bottle

Rolling pin

Ice cream

Orange

1. The lunch box has the shape of a sphere.
2. The strawberry ice cream is inside a brown coloured cone.
3. Another cone-shaped object is an orange.
4. The microwave has the shape of a cuboid.
5. There are three cylindrical-shaped objects.

C. Circle the correct option.

1. 

Cone
Cube
Cuboid

2. 
Sphere
Cube
Cone

3. 
Sphere
Cylinder
Cone

4. 
Cone
Sphere
Cylinder

5. 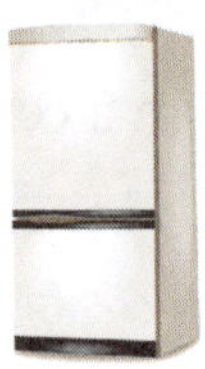
Cone
Cube
Cuboid

6. 
Cube
Sphere
Cuboid

D. Complete the patterns.

1. 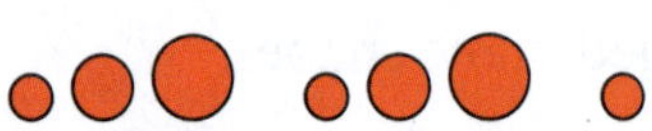 _____, _____

2.  _____, _____

3. A, B, A, B, A, _____, _____

4. X, Y, Z, X, Y, Z, _____, _____, _____

5. 90, 80, 70, _____, _____, _____ **Rule:** The number ___ is subtracted each time.

SKILL UP!

A. 21 CS Creativity and Innovation | EL | AI | STEAM CHALLENGE

Take matchsticks and make shapes involving squares, rectangles and triangles.

Look at the example shown below.

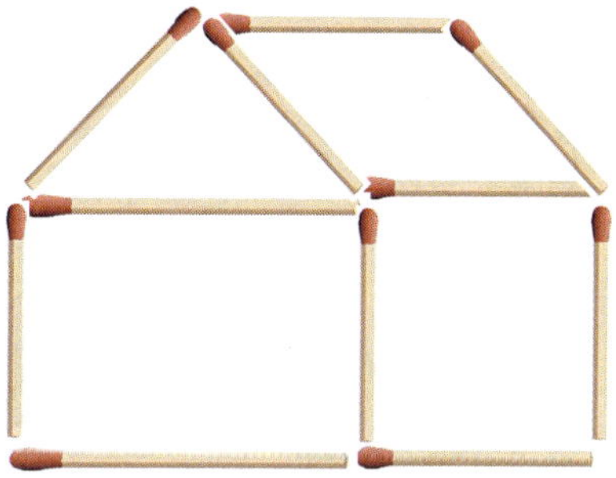

B. 21 CS Critical Thinking, Life Skills | HQ Harmony In The Self

Make a pattern with some students standing in a line holding hands.

Should we add another boy or a girl to complete the pattern?

If we do not complete the pattern, would the girl standing at the end feel left out? Why or why not?

C. 21 CS Critical Thinking, Information Literacy | EL

What happens when we combine two or more cubes?

It becomes a ____________.

D. Which flat shape is used in making of this toy box for kids? ____________

SUSTAINABLE DEVELOPMENT GOALS

Question B is in line with SDG 17 Partnerships for the Goals. It talks about partnerships between students. If one person is left out during any event, the common goal can not be achieved. In this case, the pattern can not be completed. On a bigger scale, imagine the whole country having a tree plantation drive to achieve SDG 15. But your society or your village is left out during this tree plantation drive. Other societies and villages have more trees than yours. The main goal of planting trees all over the country can not be completed. Partnerships from all are required to achieve any common goal (SDG 17).

WORKSHEET 10

21 CS Creativity and Innovation AI

Colour the horse below using the colours of your choice to get a beautiful pattern.

Reasoning Worksheet 2

1. **Which product is the greatest?**

   a. 2×5 b. 2×4 c. 3×10 d. 5×7

2. **If one pencil costs ₹3, what will be the cost of two pencils? Tick (✓) the correct options.**

   a. ₹3 b. More than ₹3 c. Less than ₹3 d. ₹6

3. **If Samir wants to colour 8 pages of a colouring book equally in 4 days, how many pages he should colour every day?**

   a. 3 pages b. 4 pages
   c. 8 pages d. 2 pages

4. **If I can put 2 kg of flour in 1 jar, how many jars will I need for 4 kg of flour?**

   a. 3 jars b. 2 jars
   c. 1 jar d. 4 jars

5. **If I put two teaspoons of sugar in my tea, how many tablespoons will be needed to put the same quantity of sugar?**

Teaspoon

Tablespoon

   a. More than 2 b. Less than 2
   c. More than half d. Equal to 2

6. **If all the sides of a rectangle are equal, it will become a:**

   a. Square b. Triangle c. Cuboid d. Cube

7. **If we join 2 cubes, it will become a:**

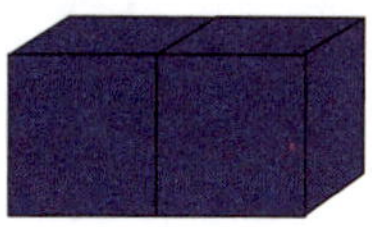

   a. Cube b. Square
   c. Rectangle d. Cuboid

8. **Which rule is followed in the number pattern formed by the cubes given below?**

   a. Start from 1 and add 2 every time
   b. Start from 1 and add 4 every time
   c. Start from 1 and add 3 every time
   d. Start from 1 and add 1 every time

11 Money

Learning Objectives

- To learn how to combine different notes and coins for given amounts
- To learn about Indian currency and rupee symbol
- To add, subtract and compare different amounts of money
- To solve word problems

Let's Get Started

21 CS Critical Thinking, Life Skills

Pinky went to purchase a teddy bear, a doll and a frock. Calculate the amount of money spent by Pinky on each item as given below.

Note

The symbol '₹' is used to represent Rupee in India.

The cost of the teddy bear is ₹ ______.

The cost of the doll is ₹ ______.

The cost of the frock is ₹ ______.

Money is needed to buy things. We have notes and coins of different values. Every country has its own currency, which is made of notes and coins. The currency used for money in India is **rupees**.

Do you know?

Currency used in Japan is **Yen**.
Currency used in Britain is **Pound**.
Currency used in America is **US dollars**.
Currency used in China is **Yuan**.
Find out the currencies used in five other countries.

Indian Rupee

The Indian currency is called rupees and paise. The value of each note is written on both the sides. Following are some currency notes used in India.

2 rupees 5 rupees 10 rupees 20 rupees 50 rupees

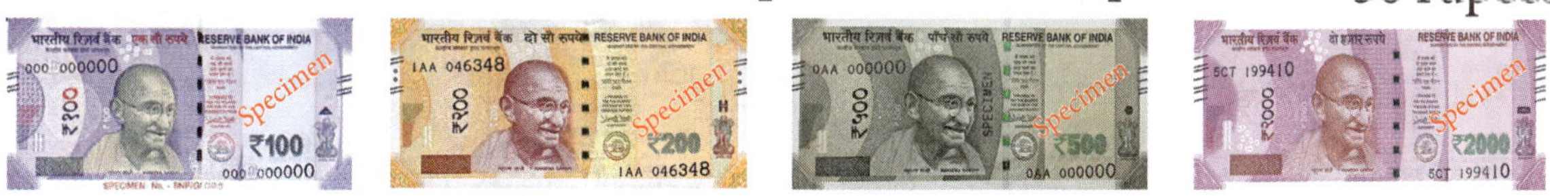

100 rupees 200 rupees 500 rupees 2000 rupees

In India, we use the following coins. The value of each coin is written only on one side.

50 paise 1 rupee 2 rupees 5 rupees 10 rupees 20 rupees

ADDITION AND SUBTRACTION OF MONEY

When we go to a shop, we pay the shopkeeper for the things we buy. This often requires us to add or subtract money. We can add or subtract money in the same way as we add or subtract other numbers.

Examples:

1. Find the total amount of money in each case.

a.  = ₹10 + ₹5 + ₹1 = ₹16

b. 

= ₹500 + ₹100 + ₹50 = ₹650

2. Subtract the following:

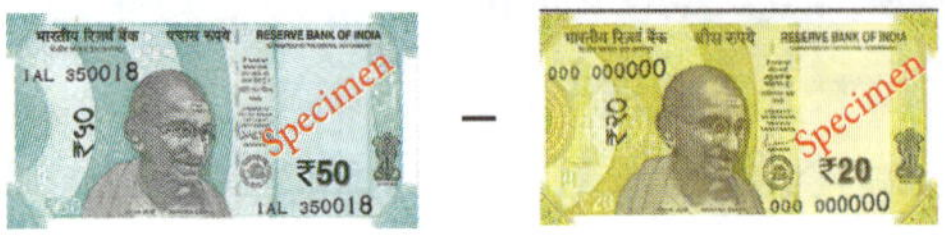 = ₹50 – ₹20 = ₹30

Comparing Money

We can compare the amounts of money just like we compare numbers.
Arya bought a video game for

 = ₹650

Naina bought another video game for

 = ₹610

Whose video game was cheaper comparatively?

As 610 < 650, Naina's video game was comparatively cheaper.

EXERCISE 11A

1. Find the total amount of money in each case.

a.  = ₹____

b.  = ₹____

c.  = ₹____

d. 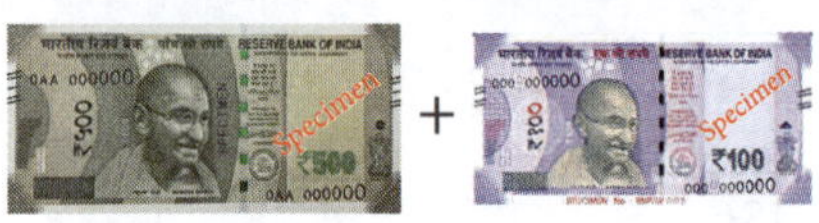 = ₹____

2. Compare the amounts of money using >, < or = .

a. 

b. 

c. 

d. 

WORD PROBLEMS

Example 1: Samira bought a dress for ₹250 and a pair of shoes for ₹125. How much money did she spend?

Solution: Cost of dress = $\ \ 250$

Cost of shoes = $+\ 125$

$\qquad\qquad\qquad\quad 375$

She spent ₹375.

Example 2: A book costs ₹395. A pen costs ₹75. Which item costs more and by how much?

Solution: Cost of book = $\ \ 395$

Cost of pen = $-\ \ 75$

$\qquad\qquad\qquad\quad 320$

The book costs ₹320 more than the pen.

EXERCISE 11B

1. **A shirt costs ₹520 and a book costs ₹270. How much do both the things cost?**

   Both the things cost ₹__________.

2. **Ehbok has ₹990. Rajesh has ₹870. How much more money does Ehbok have than Rajesh?**

   Ehbok has ₹__________ more than Rajesh.

3. **I want to buy a toy aeroplane for ₹330. If I give the shopkeeper ₹350, how much money will he return?**

   The shopkeeper will return ₹__________.

4. **Two children are saving money to watch a movie. Each movie ticket costs ₹440. How much money will they need to save?**

   They need to save ₹__________.

Go Easy!

To add different amounts of money, start counting from the greatest amount.

Example: Here we are given some amounts of notes and coins. We will start counting from ₹500 note, then ₹100 note, ₹50 note and then ₹10 coin, for making calculations simpler.

Mental Maths

1. If Radhika saves ₹100 every month, how much money will she save in 6 months? ₹__________
2. Kapil and Sunil both have ₹200 each. What is the total amount of money they have altogether? ₹__________
3.  + 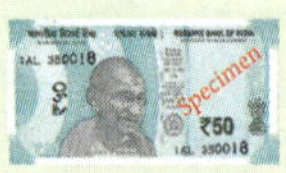 +  +  = ₹__________

Maths Lab Activity

21 CS Collaboration, Life Skills · EL · HQ Happiness My Goal

Aim: To understand addition, subtraction and comparison of money

Materials required: Toys of various kinds like dolls, teddy bears, aeroplane, etc.

Procedure: It is 'Toy Day' in school.

1. Arrange the class into 2 groups – Group A and Group B
2. Let Group A be the team of sellers. Let Group B be the team of buyers.

₹330	₹75	₹50	₹150	₹200

3. Some of the toys for sale by Group A are given.
   a. Nick is a buyer from Group B. He wishes to buy a ball and a car. How much money will he need to buy both the items? ₹__________
   b. Nina wants to buy the cheapest toy. Which toy would she be able to buy?
   ____

c. Buying a teddy bear and a doll is costlier than buying a ball and an aeroplane. True or False. __________

d. Give a combination of notes or coins that can be used by Nick and Nina to buy the toys that they wish to buy.

Combination of notes and coins:

Concept Map

Money

- Making combinations of notes and coins
- Adding the amounts of money
- Subtracting the amounts of money
- Word problems
  - find the cost
  - how much money

Key Concepts

- **Money** is available in the form of currency notes and coins.
- **Currency** is a term used to represent money. Indian currency is **rupees.**
- ₹ is the symbol of Indian rupees.
- By adding, subtracting and comparing money in real life, we can solve word problems.

A. Fill in the blanks using > or <.

1.  +  ☐ 

2.  ☐  +  + 

B. Find the total amount of money in each case.

1.  + 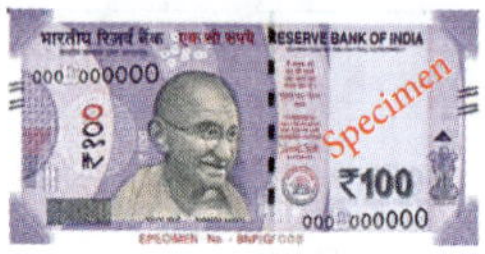 +  = ₹______

2.  +  +  = ₹______

C. Solve the following word problems.

1. Anil has ₹240 and Sunil has ₹510. How much money do they have altogether?
   Together, they both have ₹____________.
2. A shirt costs ₹230. How much will 2 such shirts cost?
   2 such shirts will cost ₹____________.

3. A chair costs ₹659. A lamp costs ₹445. How much more does the chair cost than the lamp?
   The chair costs ___________ more than the lamp.

4. Neena has ₹97 in her wallet. She decided to buy an ice cream for ₹35. How much money is left with her? Express the remaining amount in a combination of notes and coins in the space provided.

Combination of notes and coins

Skill up!

A. 21 CS Creativity and Innovation, Collaboration | EL

The students can work in groups to make ten different combinations of ₹100 using the following sets of combinations of notes and coins.

1. 4 notes of 20
2. 4 notes of 10
3. 6 notes of 5
4. 10 coins of 2
5. 10 coins of 1

B. 21 CS Critical Thinking, Life Skills | HQ Cooperation and Collaborative Living

Megha, Radha and Sneha went to buy some doughnuts. Megha had ₹50. Radha had ₹60 and Sneha had ₹45. The cost of one doughnut is ₹50.

2 ZERO HUNGER

1. Who will be able to buy the doughnut? __________
2. Do you think Sneha will be able to buy a doughnut? __________
3. How much more money does she need to buy a doughnut? ₹__________
4. Can Megha or Radha help Sneha to buy a doughnut? __________
5. Who can help her? __________
6. Do you think we should help people in need? __________

C. 21 CS Critical Thinking, Information Literacy | HQ Knowing My Needs

Pinky went to a salon for haircut and head massage. The cost of haircut service is ₹450. The cost of head massage service is ₹200.

Pinky has ₹600 in her wallet. Will she be able to take both the services?

SUSTAINABLE DEVELOPMENT GOALS

Question B is in line with SDG 2 Zero Hunger. Helping a hungry friend is a good deed. SDG 2 talks about it. It says that no one should be left hungry. There are many children in the world who do not get to eat. Think about those children and what you can do to help them.

Also, discuss whether Megha, Radha and Sneha should have bought fruits instead of doughnuts. Which is the better food and why?

WORKSHEET 11

21 CS Critical Thinking, Life Skills | HQ Harmony In The Self

Sometimes, different shops have different prices for the same item. We must always compare the prices before buying and buy from the shop that charges less. This way, we can save some money. Out of this money, we can help those who are in need.

Item	Shop A	Shop B
1. 	₹ 130	₹ 165
2. 	₹ 256	₹ 324

For the same shirt and trousers, Shop A and Shop B have different prices.

1. What is the total amount you would pay to Shop A and Shop B?

   Total Amount: Shop A __________ Shop B __________

2. How much would you save if you buy the shirt and trouser from Shop A?

   ____

3. That amount ₹__________, you can give to someone who does not have enough money to eat food.

12 Time

Learning Objectives

- To read and write the time to half past the hour
- To learn the names of the days of a week and the months of a year
- To learn about the seasons of the year and their sequence

Let's Get Started

21 CS Critical Thinking, Information Literacy

We learnt about the minute hand, hour hand and the second hand in Class 1.

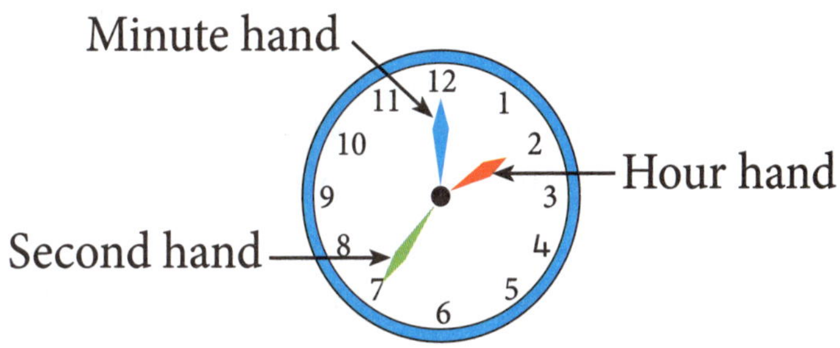

The longest hand is the second hand.
The short hand is the minute hand.
The shortest hand is the hour hand.

The activities in a school are scheduled as given below. Draw the hands on the clocks to show the given time.

Prayer time (7:00)	Sports training (9:00)	Break (11:00)	Dance class (1:00)
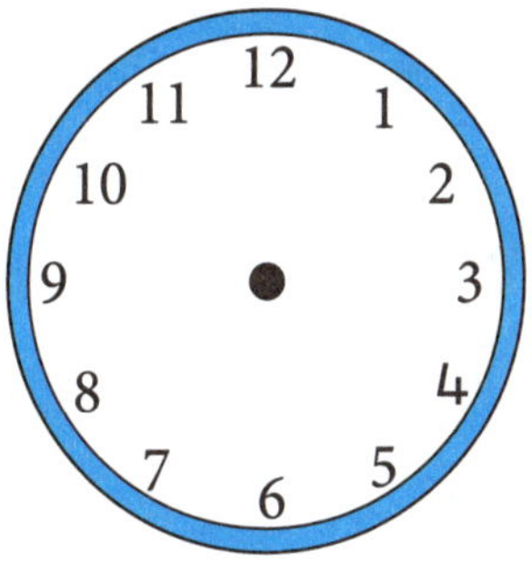	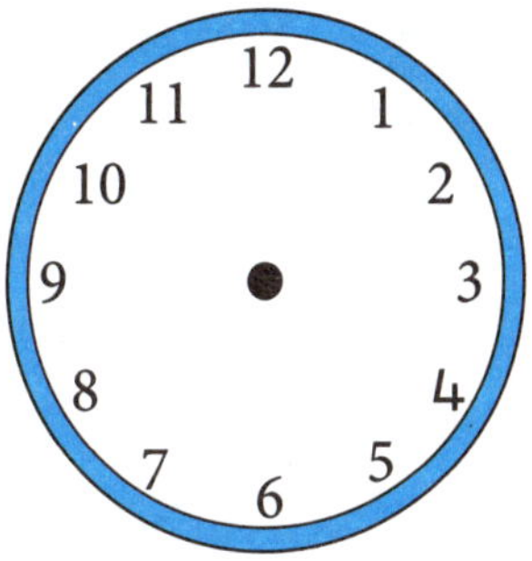		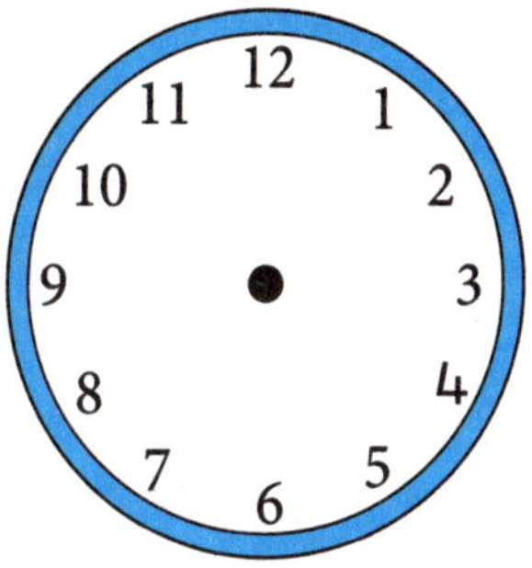

READING TIME TO HALF PAST THE HOUR

We know that a clock tells us exactly what time of the day it is.

The minute hand takes one hour to go around the clock.

In this one hour, the hour hand goes from one number to the next number.

If the minute hand starts from 12, goes around the clock from the right side and reaches 12 again, it means one hour is completed.

If the minute hand starts from 12 and reaches 6, it means half an hour is completed.

NOTE

The minute hand moves faster than the hour hand.

COMMON ERRORS

6.30 6:30

The minute hand is at 6.
The hour hand is in-between 2 and 3.
It is read as **half past two** or two thirty.
It is written as 2:30.

The minute hand is at 6.
The hour hand is in-between 5 and 6.
It is read as **half past five** or five thirty.
It is written as 5:30.

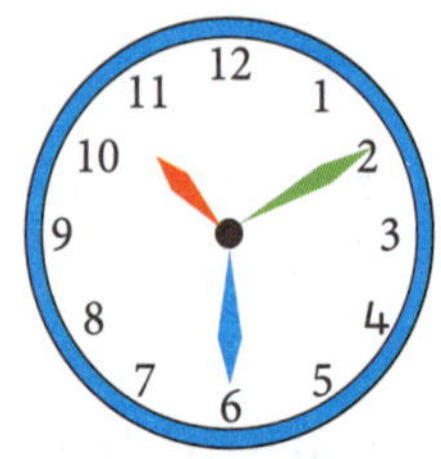

The minute hand is at 6.
The hour hand is in-between 10 and 11.
It is read as **half past ten** or ten thirty.
It is written as 10:30.

EXERCISE 12A

1. Write the time shown in the clocks.

a. 

b. 

c. 

d. 

2. Draw the hour hand and the minute hand to show the given time.

a. 12:30 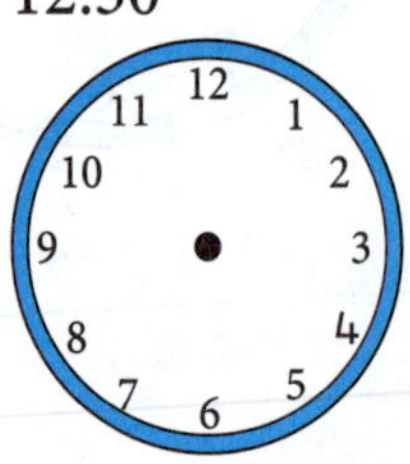

b. 4:30 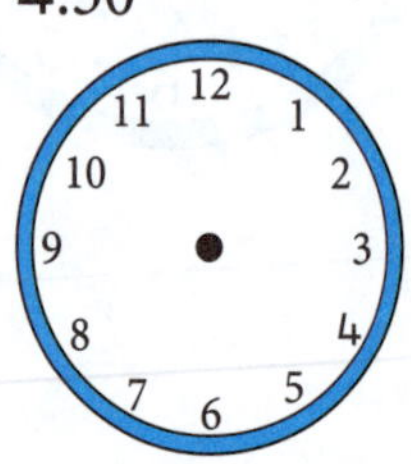

c. 6:30 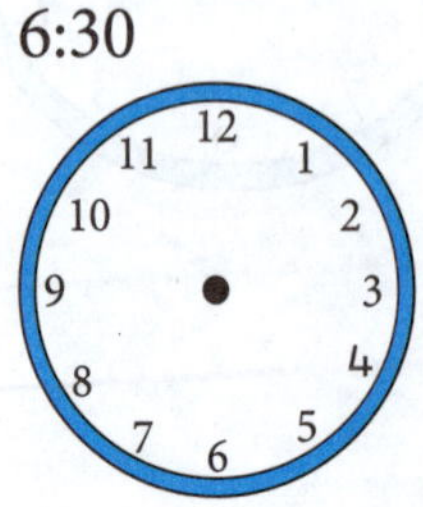

d. 8:30 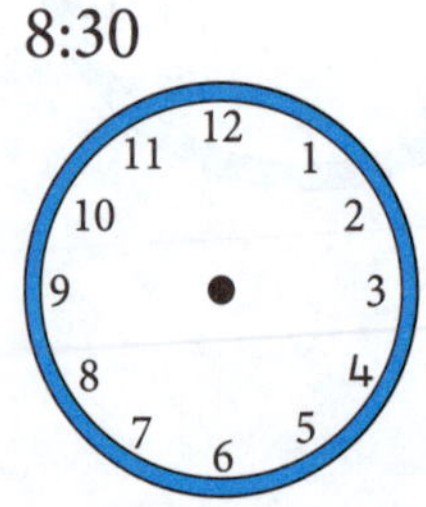

3. **Given below is the school time table of Class 2.**

Answer the following.

a. The students reach the school at __________.

b. The teacher teaches the class at __________.

c. The students have lunch together at __________.

d. The students get half an hour break to play at __________.
   When will the break get over? __________.

e. The students reach home and meet their parents at __________.

DAYS OF A WEEK

There are seven days in a week. Let us look at the order of these days.

Days of the week	Monday	Tuesday	Wednesday	Thursday	Friday	Saturday	Sunday
Order of days	First	Second	Third	Fourth	Fifth	Sixth	Seventh

Sam and Rohan are school friends. John and Neha are siblings.

Monday	Wednesday	Thursday	Friday	Sunday
 Sam	 Rohan	 John	 Neha	 John and Neha

a. Who went to school on Monday? ________

b. On which day did the siblings go for cycling? ________

c. Neha studied for her exam on ________.

d. Rohan felt sick and went to the doctor on ________.

e. ________ is seen to be swimming. Which day of the week is it? ________

Yesterday, Today and Tomorrow

We all know that today is the present day.

If today is Saturday, then the day before was Friday and the day after will be a Sunday.

The day before is called **yesterday**.

The day after is called **tomorrow**.

Friday (Yesterday)	Saturday (Today)	Sunday (Tomorrow)

So, if today is Saturday, then yesterday was Friday and tomorrow will be Sunday.

Exercise 12B

1. **Match the following.**

a. Number of days in a week	Saturday
b. The day just after Tuesday	Tuesday
c. This day comes just before Sunday	Friday
d. Yesterday was Monday, then today is	Seven
e. Today is Thursday, then tomorrow will be	Wednesday

2. **Fill in the blanks.**
   a. __________ is the last day of the week.
   b. __________ is two days before Thursday.
   c. __________ is the fourth day of the week.
   d. Tomorrow will be __________, if today is Saturday.

3. **Pinky's class test took place on Monday. Her teacher announced the results two days after the test. On which day did the students get their results?** __________

MentalMaths

1. Tomorrow will be ____________, if yesterday was Monday.
2. If today is Monday, then the day after tomorrow will be ____________.
3. The fifth day of the week is __________.
4. The number of days in 3 weeks is __________.
5. 7:30 is read as __________ or __________.

MONTHS OF THE YEAR

There are 12 months in a year. Let us look at their order and the number of days in each month.

Months	Order	Number of days
JANUARY	First	31
FEBRUARY	Second	28 or 29
MARCH	Third	31
APRIL	Fourth	30
MAY	Fifth	31
JUNE	Sixth	30
JULY	Seventh	31
AUGUST	Eighth	31
SEPTEMBER	Ninth	30
OCTOBER	Tenth	31
NOVEMBER	Eleventh	30
DECEMBER	Twelfth	31

A year has 365 days.

MentalMaths

1. Which two consecutive months have 31 days?
2. The only month which does not have 30 or 31 days is __________.

NOTE

1. February has 28 days. But, in a leap year, it has 29 days. Leap year comes after every 4 years. A leap year has 366 days.
2. February is the shortest month of the year.
3. Months have 30 or 31 days, alternatively.

Go Easy!

Let us learn the names of 12 months using our fists.

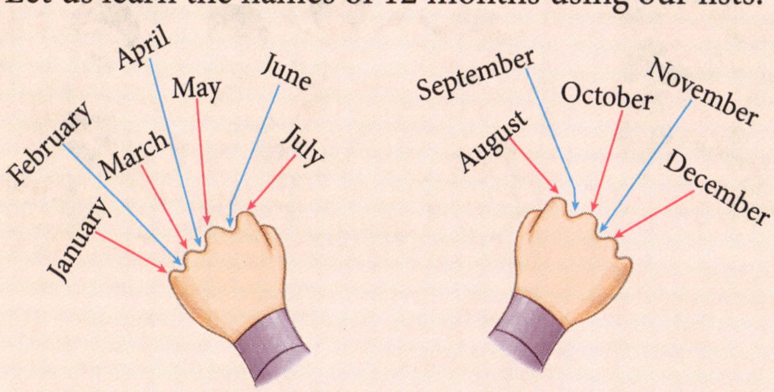

Did you find any pattern? The months counted on the knuckles have 31 days and the months counted on the grooves have 30 days (28 or 29 days for February).

Learn the months by counting them on the knuckles and the grooves. Do not count the thumb knuckle.

DO YOU KNOW?

July was named after Julius Caesar, the Roman Politician and Military General. Augustus Caesar was grandnephew of Julius Caesar who came into power after Julius and the month of August was named after him.

SEASONS OF THE YEAR

There are five seasons in a year. Let us learn about them.

Winter

It is a very cold season. Snowfall happens in some areas during this season. People usually wear jackets, sweaters and other woollen clothes.

Spring

Spring comes after winter. New plants grow, flowers blossom and new leaves grow in this season. Weather starts to warm up.

Summer

It is a very hot season. Summer season comes after the spring season. People usually wear cotton clothes.

Monsoon (Rainy)

Sky gets covered with dark clouds. It rains with thunderstorms. Surroundings get wet and cools the atmosphere. People wear raincoats and use umbrellas. A rainbow is seen sometimes when the rain stops.

Autumn

It is a pleasant season. The leaves change colour. They start falling from trees so that new leaves can come in spring. Autumn comes before winter.

Exercise 12C

1. Match the following.

a. The third month of the year	November
b. The month just before August	June
c. The month not having 30 or 31 days	July
d. December comes after this month	February
e. The sixth month of the year	March

2. Fill in the blanks.

a. Months that have 30 days are ______________________________

b. Name your birthday month. ____________

c. Which day is it in the present year? ____________

d. Trees shed their leaves in the ____________ season

e. The season in which people usually wear cotton clothes is ____________.

f. People wear sweaters and jackets in the ____________ season.

g. The weather in autumn is ____________.

h. People wear raincoats in the ____________ season.

3. Name the following seasons.

a. Hot season ________

b. Pleasant season ________

c. Cold season ________

d. New leaves come in this season ________

e. Wet surroundings ________

MentalMaths

Look at the calendar and answer the questions.

1. How many days are there in February 2022? [ ]

2. What is the total number of Saturdays in February? [ ]

3. Is 2022 a leap year? (Yes/No) [ ]

FEBRUARY

S	M	T	W	T	F	S
		1	2	3	4	5
6	7	8	9	10	11	12
13	14	15	16	17	18	19
20	21	22	23	24	25	26
27	28					

MATHS LAB ACTIVITY

21 CS Information Literacy EL

Aim: To identify the days and months of the year

Materials required: A calendar

Procedure:

1. Think of some special days in a year like

Republic Day	Independence Day	Mahatma Gandhi's birthday
Children's Day	Christmas	New Year's Day

2. Mark all the above days in the calendar.
3. Write the day on which each of them will fall in the space given below.

Republic Day	____________	Independence Day	____________
Mahatma Gandhi's birthday	____________	Children's Day	____________
Christmas	____________	New Year's Day	____________

CONCEPT MAP

Time

- Read and write the time to half past the hour

- **Days of the week**
  Monday, Tuesday, Wednesday, Thursday, Friday, Saturday, Sunday
- **Months of the year**
  January, February, March, April, May, June, July, August, September, October, November, December
- **Seasons**
  Winter, Spring, Summer, Monsoon, Autumn

Key Concepts

- When the minute hand starts from 12 and reaches 6, it means half an hour is completed.
- There are 7 days in a week.
- There are 12 months in a year. February has 28 days.
- A year has 365 days and a leap has 366 days.
- February has 29 days in a leap year.
- There are 5 seasons in a year.

CROSSWORD

Fill in the crossword given below after studying the clues.

Across

1. The short hand of a clock is called the _______ hand.
2. The month after May
3. The month after March
5. The day after today

Down

1. The first day of the week
2. The day after Wednesday
3. 10:30 is read as ________ past 10.
4. The season when we feel very hot

A. Fill in the blanks.

1. Half past 11 is written as ______________. (11:00/11:30)
2. There are ______________ days in a week. (7/8)
3. If yesterday was Thursday, then today is ______________. (Wednesday/Friday)
4. Flowers bloom in the ______________ season. (spring/winter)

B. Draw the hour hand on the clocks to show the given time.

1. 7:30

2. 11:30

3. 9:30

4. 3:30

C. Write T for true and F for false.

1. When the minute hand starts from 12 and reaches at 5, half an hour is completed. ☐
2. Three days after Wednesday is Saturday. ☐
3. Monday is the last day of the week. ☐
4. Thursday comes after Tuesday. ☐
5. There are 30 days in February. ☐

D. Look at the 2021 calendar below and answer the following questions.

2021

JANUARY

Mo	Tu	We	Th	Fr	Sa	Su
				1	2	3
4	5	6	7	8	9	10
11	12	13	14	15	16	17
18	19	20	21	22	23	24
25	26	27	28	29	30	31

FEBRUARY

Mo	Tu	We	Th	Fr	Sa	Su
1	2	3	4	5	6	7
8	9	10	11	12	13	14
15	16	17	18	19	20	21
22	23	24	25	26	27	28

MARCH

Mo	Tu	We	Th	Fr	Sa	Su
1	2	3	4	5	6	7
8	9	10	11	12	13	14
15	16	17	18	19	20	21
22	23	24	25	26	27	28
29	30	31				

APRIL

Mo	Tu	We	Th	Fr	Sa	Su
			1	2	3	4
5	6	7	8	9	10	11
12	13	14	15	16	17	18
19	20	21	22	23	24	25
26	27	28	29	30		

MAY

Mo	Tu	We	Th	Fr	Sa	Su
					1	2
3	4	5	6	7	8	9
10	11	12	13	14	15	16
17	18	19	20	21	22	23
24	25	26	27	28	29	30
31						

JUNE

Mo	Tu	We	Th	Fr	Sa	Su
	1	2	3	4	5	6
7	8	9	10	11	12	13
14	15	16	17	18	19	20
21	22	23	24	25	26	27
28	29	30				

JUJY

Mo	Tu	We	Th	Fr	Sa	Su
			1	2	3	4
5	6	7	8	9	10	11
12	13	14	15	16	17	18
19	20	21	22	23	24	25
26	27	28	29	30	31	

AUGUST

Mo	Tu	We	Th	Fr	Sa	Su
						1
2	3	4	5	6	7	8
9	10	11	12	13	14	15
16	17	18	19	20	21	22
23	24	25	26	27	28	29
30	31					

SEPTEMBER

Mo	Tu	We	Th	Fr	Sa	Su
		1	2	3	4	5
6	7	8	9	10	11	12
13	14	15	16	17	18	19
20	21	22	23	24	25	26
27	28	29	30			

OCTOBER

Mo	Tu	We	Th	Fr	Sa	Su
				1	2	3
4	5	6	7	8	9	10
11	12	13	14	15	16	17
18	19	20	21	22	23	24
25	26	27	28	29	30	31

NOVEMBER

Mo	Tu	We	Th	Fr	Sa	Su
1	2	3	4	5	6	7
8	9	10	11	12	13	14
15	16	17	18	19	20	21
22	23	24	25	26	27	28
29	30					

DECEMBER

Mo	Tu	We	Th	Fr	Sa	Su
		1	2	3	4	5
6	7	8	9	10	11	12
13	14	15	16	17	18	19
20	21	22	23	24	25	26
27	28	29	30	31		

1. Which months have 5 Sundays?

   ____

2. Which day falls on 2nd April?

   ____

3. Name the month that comes in between April and June.

   ____

4. Independence Day comes on 15th August every year. On which day does it fall in 2021?

   ____

SKILL UP!

3 GOOD HEALTH AND WELL-BEING

A. 21 CS Information Literacy, Life Skills

Make a time table of your daily routine after coming home from school.

Lunch	Playing	Studying	Dinner	Sleeping

B. 21 CS Life Skills HQ Knowing My Needs

Rahul has a routine of doing his self-study at 5:30 in the evening.

He has a class test on Thursday.

On Tuesday, he went to play cricket at 5 o'clock and returned home at 7:30. He could not spend time on self-study on Tuesday.

On Wednesday, he again went to play. He returned home at 7 o'clock. He again could not spend time on self-study.

On Thursday, he did not perform well in the class test.

Do you know why?

How should he set his time table to study as well as play cricket?

Do you think we should practise the class lessons at home?

Do you think time is precious?

C. 21 CS Critical Thinking

Kriti decided to eat two apples every day. She had ten apples. If she starts eating apples from Tuesday, which day will she be able to finish the apples?

SUSTAINABLE DEVELOPMENT GOALS

All questions on this page are in line with SDG 3 Good Health and Well-Being. These questions will tell you about the importance of good health and well-being.

If you have a good daily routine, play well, rest well, eat good food, you will have good health.

WORKSHEET 12

21 CS Information Literacy | CC Integration with General Knowledge

Name the seasons. What special features do you see in these seasons? Sequence the seasons from 1 to 5 in the space provided. One has been done for you.

1. 

Name:

Features:

[ ]

2. 

Name:

Features:

[ ]

3. 

Name:

Features:

[1]

4. 

Name:

Features:

[ ]

5. 

Name:

Features:

[ ]

13 Data Handling

Learning Objectives

- To learn how to organise data and make lists
- To learn how to compare data and find results

Let's Get Started

21 CS Information Literacy | HQ Happiness My Goal

It is Nick's birthday today. Here are some balloons, a birthday cake and some doughnuts. Nick's friends are enjoying and eating ice creams at the birthday party.

1. There are _____ balloons in all.
2. The number of doughnuts is _____.
3. The number of children eating ice creams is _____.

4. The number of red balloons is _____.
5. _____ girls are wearing hats.
6. Yellow balloons are more than green balloons. True or False? _____

7. The number of candles on the cake is _____.
8. It means Nick is _____ years old now.

MAKING LISTS

When we observe objects, we can count them, observe their colours, observe their arrangements or positions, etc. It helps us to answer the questions about those objects.

Example 1: Given below are the different coloured flowers growing in Arpana's garden.

Solution:

List of flowers:

a. The number of red flowers = 5
b. The number of yellow flowers = 4
c. The number of pink flowers = 4
d. The number of purple flowers = 3
e. The number of orange flowers = 2

NOTE

Making lists helps us to organise data and then work on it in an easier way.

Answer the following questions.

a. What is the total number of flowers in Arpana's garden?
5 + 4 + 4 + 3 + 2 = 18
b. Which colour flowers are most in number?
Red
c. Which colour flowers are least in number?
Orange
d. How many more red flowers are there than the purple flowers?
2
e. Which colour flowers are equal in number?
Yellow and Pink

Example 2: The following chart shows the number of chocolate boxes a shopkeeper sold during a week.

Observe the chart and answer the questions.

Solution:

Answer the following questions.

a. What is the total number of chocolate boxes the shopkeeper sold during the week?

1 + 2 + 3 + 2 + 4 + 5 + 6 = 23

b. How many boxes of chocolates did he sell on Friday?

4

c. On which day did he sell just one box of chocolates?

Monday

d. On which day did he sell the maximum number of boxes?

Sunday

Fill in the blanks.

a. He sold ___________ boxes on Wednesday.

b. He sold ___________ boxes each on Tuesday and Thursday.

c. He sold ___________ more box on Saturday than on Friday.

Exercise 13A

1. **In one day, a shopkeeper sold the following items.**

   Observe the items and answer the questions.

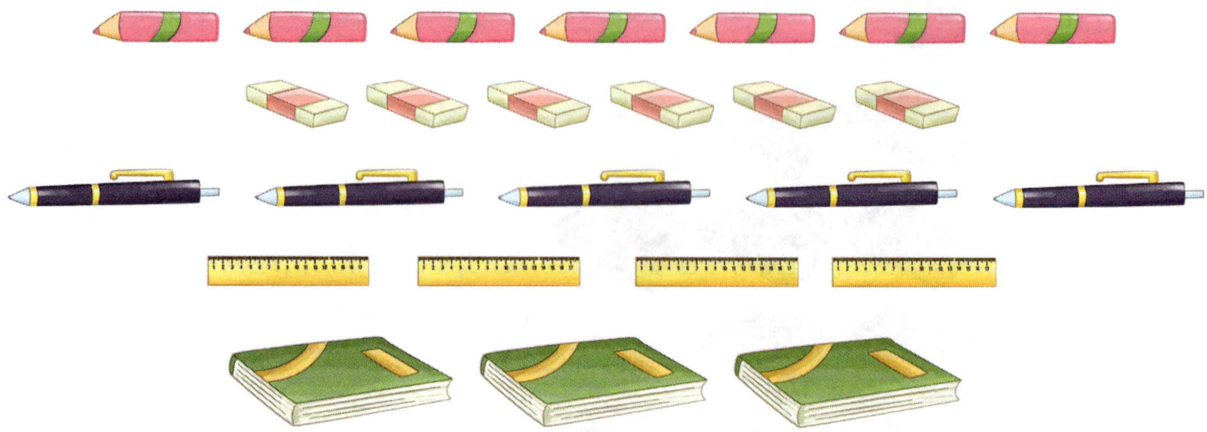

   a. Count each item sold by the shopkeeper and make a list.

   Pencils __________ Erasers __________ Pens __________

   Rulers __________ Notebooks __________

   b. What is the total number of items sold by him? __________

   c. How many more pencils did he sell than notebooks? __________

   d. Which item did he sell the most in number? __________

   e. Which item did he sell the least in number? __________

   f. How many more erasers did he sell than notebooks? __________

2. **Johny and his mother were playing with colourful blocks. They created different shapes using the blocks. Answer the following questions.**

   a. Count the number of each block and make a list.

   Red _____ Yellow _____ Blue _____ Green _____

   b. What is the total number of blocks? _____

   c. How many types of colours are used? _____

   d. The number of cubes is _____.

   e. The total number of cubes and cuboids is _____.

   f. The number of yellow-coloured blocks is _____ (less/greater) than the number of blue-coloured blocks.

MENTAL MATHS

1. Consider the pattern.

2, 2, 2, 3, 3, 3, 4, 4, 4, 5, 5, 5

a. How many numbers are there? ________

b. How many times is each number repeated? ________

2. Neha has 11 cards, Sneha has 8 cards and Meera has 16 cards.

a. If they start counting the cards simultaneously, who will be able to finish counting first? ________

b. Who has the maximum number of cards? ________

c. Find the difference between the number of cards with Neha and Sneha. ________

GO EASY!

- Data handling can become much easier if you observe data in your surroundings, say items in your school bag, in your kitchen, in your classroom and then make comparisons and find results.
- The most important thing is to make a list of all the items first.

PUZZLE!

Observe the picture. Count different objects and make a list as follows:

1. Number of trees ____
2. Number of marbles on the ground ____
3. Number of children ____
4. Number of boys ____
5. Number of girls ____
6. Number of balls ____

If there are five more marbles in the red bag carried by one of the boys in the picture, what will be the total number of marbles then?

MATHS LAB ACTIVITY

21 CS Critical Thinking, Creativity and Innovation · EL · CC Integration with English

Aim: To reinforce the concept of organising and comparing data and finding results

Materials required: A pen and a notebook

Procedure:

1. Write down the following two words in your notebook.

   Alphabetical **Education**

2. Read and write the number of vowels in these two words.

   But before proceeding, write down all the vowels of the English alphabets. _______

Words	Number of vowels
Alphabetical	5
Education	5

3. You notice that there are same number of vowels in both the words.

   Vowels in 'Alphabetical': a, a, e, i, a

   Vowels in 'Education': e, u, a, i, o

4. What do you observe?

   Which word contains all the vowels? ____________

   Which vowels are missing in the word 'Alphabetical'? ____________

5. Find out more such words which contain all the vowels of the English alphabet.

   ____________, ____________, ____________, ____________

CONCEPT MAP

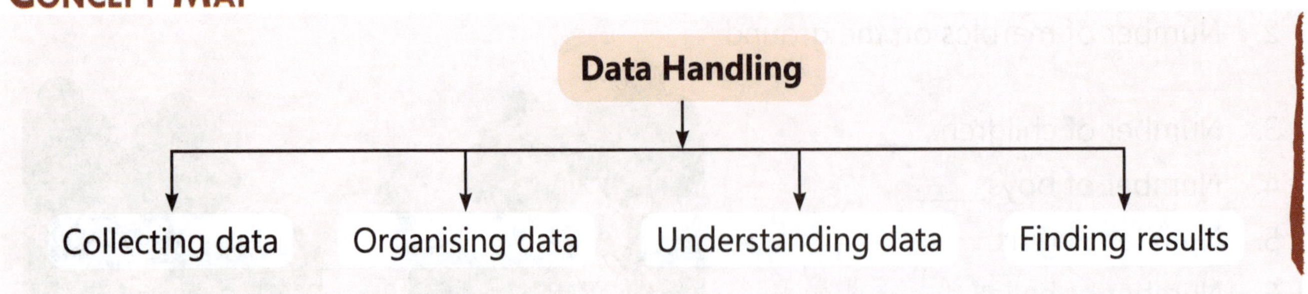

KEY CONCEPTS

- **Data** is the information collected.
- **Organising data** means placing the data in a way so that we can understand it.
- After organising data, we can prepare lists and **understand** data easily.
- Final step is to find the **results**.

Chapter Revision

A. Meena went to the market and bought the following items. Observe the items and answer the questions.

1. How many dresses did Meena buy? ____________
2. How many pens did Meena buy? ____________
3. How many more pens did Meena buy than belts? ____________
4. How many more books did Meena buy than dresses? ____________
5. How many pairs of footwear did Meena buy? ____________

B. An ice cream vendor sold the following number of ice creams during the week. Observe the chart and answer the questions.

1. List the number of ice creams sold on each day.
2. What is the total number of ice creams sold by the vendor in the whole week? ____________
3. How many more ice creams did he sell on Friday than on Monday? ____________
4. On which day did he sell the least number of ice creams? ____________
5. On which day did he sell the most number of ice creams? ____________
6. On which two days did he sell the same number of ice creams? ____________

SKILL UP!

A. 21 CS Information Literacy | HQ Happiness My Goal

Collect some stamps starting from Monday till Friday.

- List down how many stamps you collected on each day.
- Find out on which day you collected the least and the most number of stamps.
- How many stamps did you collect on Thursday and Monday?
- Was the number of stamps collected on Friday more than the number of stamps collected on Tuesday?

B. 21 CS Collaboration, Life Skills | CC Integration with Physical Education

10 REDUCED INEQUALITIES

Given here is a list of students and their hobbies.

Hobbies	Students
Dancing	Tapi, Megha, Mimi
Swimming	Renu, Jiva, Bill, Annie, Sara
Singing	Zorin

1. Count and write the number of students who like:

   Dancing ________, Swimming ________ and Singing ________

2. The teacher wants to arrange the class into two groups for dancing and swimming competitions. Who will not be able to take part in the competitions? Do you think he should be given a chance to show his talent?

C. 21 CS Critical Thinking, Information Literacy

Tanya read 7 storybooks, Manya read 5 storybooks and Kavya read 8 storybooks in 20 days. Who has the best speed in reading a storybook? Kavya read one storybook more than Tanya. Do you think Tanya has the capability to gain speed in reading? Can Tanya and Kavya be equally good in reading speed?

SUSTAINABLE DEVELOPMENT GOALS

Question B is in line with SDG 10 Reduced Inequalities. All children, boys and girls, should have the freedom to choose their hobbies. They should be able to express themselves without being told that they are a boy or a girl and they should not do this and that. Only after we are aware that boys and girls are equal (SDG 5) through quality education (SDG 4), then only we can have reduced inequalities (SDG 10).

WORKSHEET 13

21 CS Information Literacy HQ Happiness My Goal

The following is the list of students who like to watch different channels on TV.

Channel	Number of Students
Cartoon channel	15
News channel	2
Sports channel	9

Cartoon channel

News channel

Sports channel

Observe the list above and answer the questions.

a. Which channel is liked by the most number of students? __________

b. Which channel is liked by the least number of students? __________

c. How many students like to watch the sports channel? __________

d. How many more students like to watch the cartoon channel than the news channel? __________

e. Write the total number of students according to the given data above. __________

f. Three more students join the list of students liking the sports channel. How many students like the sports channel now? __________

Which is your favourite channel on TV? Name your favourite TV show.

Reasoning Worksheet 3

1. **Vidya wants to buy a doll for ₹450. She collects ₹100 every day for 5 days. Tick (✓) the correct options.**

   a. She can buy the doll for ₹590.
   b. She cannot buy the doll for ₹500.
   c. She can buy the doll for ₹500.
   d. She cannot buy the doll for ₹505.

2. **Arshad had ₹500 and Anmol had ₹300. They wanted to share a pizza which costs ₹500. Tick (✓) the correct options.**

   a. They can together buy the pizza.
   b. Arshad alone can buy the pizza.
   c. Anmol alone can buy the pizza.
   d. They cannot buy the pizza.

3. **In which month should Suklin take out woollen clothes to wear?**

   a. March b. September c. June d. December

4. **Jinnie goes to park to play for 2 hours. She goes at 5 o'clock. When should she return home?**

   a. 8 o'clock b. 7 o'clock c. 6 o'clock d. 5 o'clock

5. **Greg read the following number of pages of a storybook in 4 days.**

   Monday – 5 pages, Tuesday – 3 pages, Wednesday – 6 pages, Thursday – 2 pages

   Write T for true and F for false for the following statements.

   a. He read 18 pages in 4 days.
   b. He got more time to read on Wednesday.
   c. He got less time to read on Thursday.
   d. He read 1 page more on Tuesday than on Thursday.

Review Corner

Review 1 — Chapters 1–3

Maximum Marks = 40

A. Choose the correct option. [3 × 1]

1. The place value of 7 in 479 is

   a. 40 b. 70 c. 90 d. 700

2. 1 added to the smallest 2-digit number is

   a. 98 b. 99 c. 10 d. 11

3. The tens digit in the result of 78 – 25 is

   a. 7 b. 2 c. 6 d. 5

B. Fill in the blanks. [3 × 2]

1. Arrange the numbers in descending order.
   59, 49, 51, 54, 55

   ____

2. a. The three numbers that come in-between 87 and 91 are ______________________________.

   b. Number name for the smallest 3-digit number is ______________________________.

3. 25 subtracted from the greatest 2-digit number is ______________________________.

Rough Work

C. Solve the following. **[5 × 3]**

1. a. Write > or <.

   98 ☐ 89

   b. The sum of 45 and 1 gives ________. The result is the ________ (successor/predecessor) of 45.

	T	O
+		

   c. One hundred forty-nine in numerals is _______.

2. Subtract 45 from 87.
   Is the result an odd number?

   ____

	T	O
−		

3. Solve 24 + 53 vertically.
   Write the predecessor of the result.

   ____

	T	O
+		

4. 3 tens + 5 tens = ______. Subtract the result from 9 tens.
   Show vertical subtraction.

5. Solve 57 + 24 + 13.

	T	O
+		

Rough Work

D. Answer the following questions. [4 × 4]

1. Add the successor of 85 to 8.
   Write the number name of the result.

   ____

	T	O
+		

2. Sukher skipped 23 times on Monday and 51 times on Tuesday. How many times did Sukher skip on both these days?

	T	O
+		

3. Find the difference between 76 and 37.
   Write the place value of all the digits in the result.

	T	O
−		

4. Out of 94 books, the teacher distributed 38 books. How many books were left?

	T	O
−		

Rough Work

Maximum Marks = 40

A. Write T for true and F for false. **[3 × 1]**

1. The numeral for seven hundred nine is 790. ☐
2. The successor of 99 gives the smallest 2-digit number. ☐
3. 5 + 5 + 5 = 3 × 5 ☐

B. Answer the following questions. **[3 × 2]**

1. a. Fill in the blanks using < or >.
   349 ☐ 562

   b. 611 – 111 = ________

	H	T	O
–			

2. Write the smallest and the greatest number using the digits 0, 3 and 8.

Digits	Smallest number	Greatest number
0, 3 and 8		

3. Solve 54 × 3.

	T	O
×		

Rough Work

C. Solve the following. [5 × 3]

1. a. Write the smallest 4-digit number and write its number name.
   b. Write the place value and face value of each digit in 524.
   c. Complete the pattern: 235, 335, ____, ____, ____, ____
2. a. Write the short form of 600 + 20 + 6. Write its number name.
   b. Fill in the missing numbers on the number line.

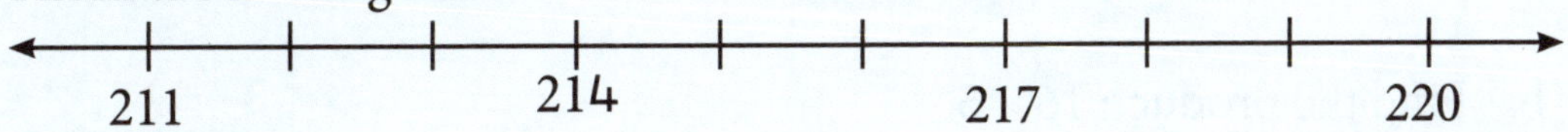

   c. Find the sum: 122 + 33 + 2.

H	T	O
+		

3. Solve 233 + 254 + 312.
   Write the number name of the result.
   ____

T	O
+	

4. Solve 87 – 28.
   Find the predecessor of the result.
   ____

T	O
–	

5. a. Write the multiplication statements for the following repeated additions.
   5 + 5 + 5 + 5 = _____ and 7 + 7 + 7 + 7 + 7 = _____
   b. Express 4 × 2 on the number line. Find the product.

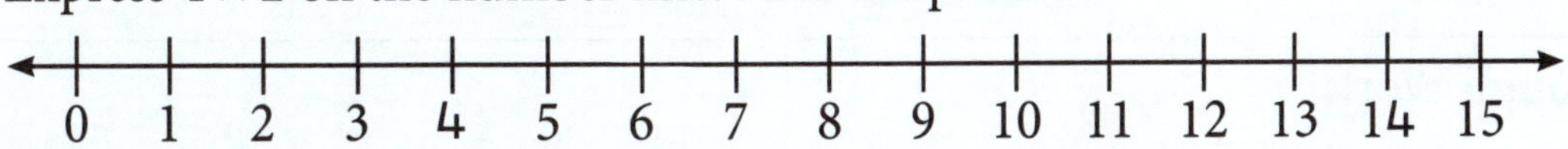

   c. Find the product of 24 and 8.

H	T	O
×		

Rough Work

D. Answer the following questions. [4 × 4]

1. a. What is the difference between 984 and 152?

H T O

−

b. Find the product: 16 × 5.

T O

×

2. There are 253 boys and 245 girls in a school. How many children are there in the school?

H T O

+

3. Out of 796 cars in a parking area, 243 cars were white in colour. How many cars were not white?

H T O

−

4. A packet contains 4 doughnuts. How many doughnuts are there in 6 such packets?

T O

×

Rough Work

Review 3 Chapters 8–10

Maximum Marks = 40

A. Match the following. [3 × 1]

1. 5 ÷ 1 — 10 cm
2. Length of a pen — square
3.  — 5

B. Fill in the blanks. [3 × 2]

1. a. 2 ÷ 2 = ______ b. 99 ÷ 0 = ______
2. a. The mass of potatoes will be measured in ______.
   b. A teaspoon measures about ______ mℓ of a liquid.
3. a. An oval has ______ straight edges and ______ corners.
   b. Complete the pattern: X, X, Z, X, X, ______, ______, ______, ______

C. Solve the following. [5 × 3]

1. Solve 8 ÷ 2 using repeated subtraction.
2. Put 6 flowers equally in 3 vases. How many flowers are there in each vase?
   Write the division statement. ________________
3. a. 1 m = ____ cm b. 1 kg = ____ g c. 1 ℓ = ____ mℓ
4. Tick (✓) the correct answer.

Rectangle/Circle

Triangle/Rectangle

Rectangle/Square

5. Complete the patterns.
   a. 2, 4, 6, 8, ______, ______, ______ b. L, M, N, O, L, M, _____, _____
   c.  ______, ______, ______

Rough Work

D. Answer the following questions. [4 × 4]

1. Solve 10 ÷ 2 using the number line.

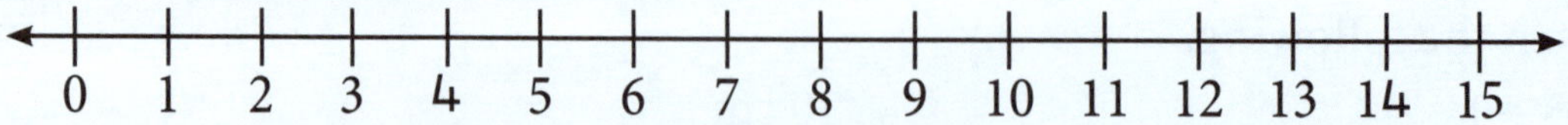

2. Sam wants to eat 12 toffees equally in 6 days. How many toffees should he eat every day?

Sam should eat _____ toffees every day.

3. a. 56 ÷ 8 = _____

   b. The length of a bed can be 3 metres. True/False

   c. Complete the pattern.

 ___________, ___________

   d. Write V for vertical line, H for horizontal line and S for slanting line.

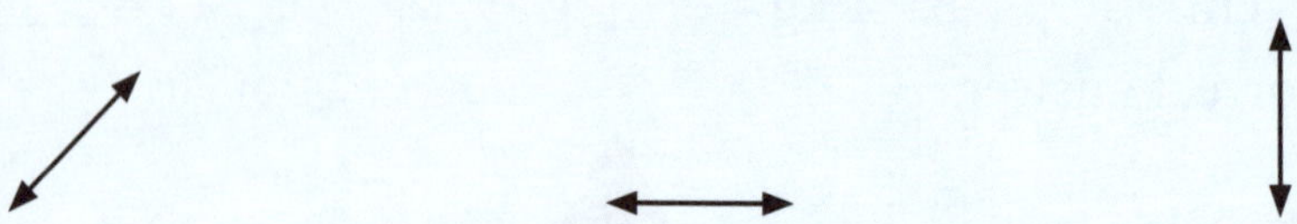

_______________ _______________ _______________

4. Write R for rolling object, S for sliding object and RS for the object that can roll as well as slide.

__________ __________ __________ __________

Rough Work

Review 4

Chapters 11–13

Maximum Marks = 40

A. Match the following. [3 × 1]

1.  — The first day of the week
2.  — ₹10

3. Monday — 5 o'clock

B. Fill in the blanks. [3 × 2]

1. a.  +  = ₹____________

   b.  +  +  = ₹____________

2. a. If today is Friday, then tomorrow will be ____________.

   b. ____________ season comes after the winter season.

3. Aayushi bought the given items. Answer the following questions.

   a. She bought ________ notebooks and ________ pens.

   b. The total number of items is ________.

C. Solve. [5 × 3]

1. Fill in the blanks using >, < or =.

   a. 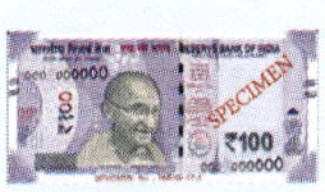 □  + 

   b.  □  + 

   c. 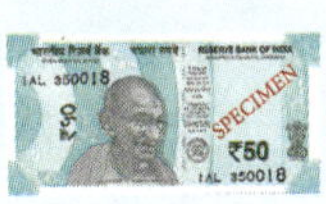 + 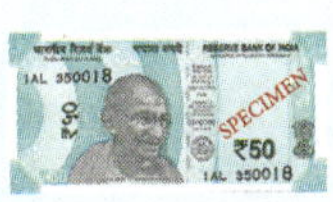 □  + 

Rough Work

2. A fruit basket costs ₹485. Give two combinations of notes and coins that can be given by Sharda to the fruit seller.

3. a. Look at the clock given below. I went to my friend's house at __________.

   b. July has __________ days.

   c. Snowfall is seen at some places during the __________ season.

4. Meg and Jon drank 6 glasses of juice on Monday, 5 glasses on Tuesday and 6 glasses on Wednesday.

   a. On which two days did they drink the same amount of juice? __________

   b. The sum of the number of juice glasses on Monday and Tuesday is __________.

   c. How many glasses of juice did they drink on all the three days? __________

5. Consider the pattern.

   3, 3, 3, 4, 4, 4, 4, 5, 5, 5, 5, 5, 5

   a. How many times is each number repeated? __________

   b. How many numbers are there? __________

   c. 5 occurs five times and 3 occurs thrice. True or False? __________

Rough Work

D. Answer the following questions. [4 × 4]

1. A toy bus costs ₹380 and a toy aeroplane costs ₹590. Which toy costs more and by how much?
2. a. I purchased a dress for ₹870. I gave the shopkeeper ₹990.
   How much money will I get in return from the shopkeeper?

   b. What kind of clothes do we wear in summer season? (Woollen, Cotton, Raincoats)
3. a. I reached the market at 5:00 in the evening. I left the market after one hour. Draw the hands of the clock to show the time when I left the market.

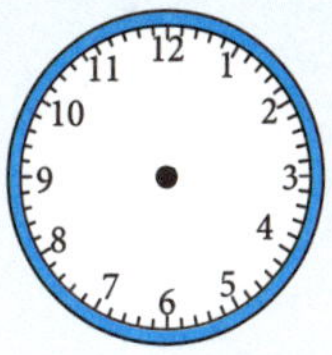

   b. Write the names of the third, seventh and tenth months of the year.
4. An ice cream vender sold the following ice creams in one day.

Vanilla	5
Chocolate	8
Mango	7
Strawberry	9

   a. Which ice cream did he sell the most in number?

   b. Which flavours of ice creams did he sell more than Mango?

   c. Which ice cream did he sell the least in number?

   d. What is the total number of ice creams that he sold?

Rough Work

CLASS 2

QUESTION PAPER SET A

IMO

SOF INTERNATIONAL MATHEMATICS OLYMPIAD 2020-21

DO NOT OPEN THIS BOOKLET UNTIL ASKED TO DO SO

Total Questions: 35 | Time: 1 hr.

Guidelines for the Candidate

1. You will get additional ten minutes to fill up information about yourself on the OMR Sheet, before the start of the exam.
2. Write your **Name, School Code, Class, Section, Roll No.** and **Mobile Number** clearly on the **OMR Sheet** and do not forget to sign it. We will share your marks / result and other information related to SOF exams on your mobile number.
3. The Question Paper comprises four sections:

   Logical Reasoning (10 Questions), **Mathematical Reasoning** (10 Questions), **Everyday Mathematics** (10 Questions) and **Achievers Section** (5 Questions)

   Each question in Achievers Section carries 2 marks, whereas all other questions carry one mark each.
4. All questions are compulsory. There is no negative marking. Use of calculator is not permitted.
5. There is only ONE correct answer. Choose only ONE option for an answer.
6. To mark your choice of answers by darkening the circles on the OMR Sheet, use **HB Pencil** or **Blue / Black ball point pen** only. E.g.

   Q.16: Sonia had 80 sweets. She gave 15 sweets to Danish and 15 sweets to Megha. How many sweets are left with her?

   A. 50 B. 30 C. 60 D. 40

   As the correct answer is option A, you must darken the circle corresponding to option A on the OMR Sheet. 16. ● Ⓑ Ⓒ Ⓓ
7. Rough work should be done in the blank space provided in the booklet.
8. Return the OMR Sheet to the invigilator at the end of the exam.
9. Please fill in your personal details in the space provided on this page before attempting the paper.

SCIENCE OLYMPIAD FOUNDATION

Inspiring Young Minds Through Knowledge Olympiads

Name:..

Section:........... SOF Olympiad Roll No.:.. Contact No.:...

1. Which of the following figures is exactly same as the given figure?

A. 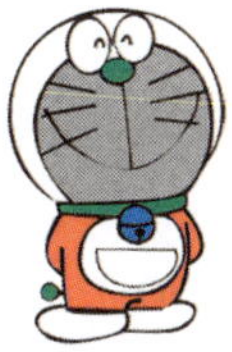 B.  C.  D. 

---

2. If  is related to 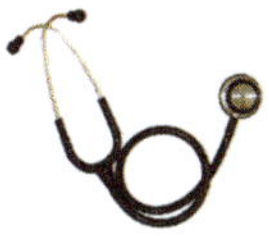 in some way, then in the same way  is related to ______.

A.  B.  C. 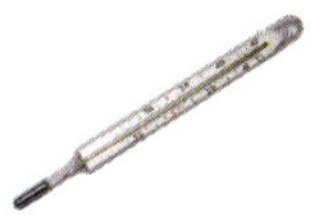 D. 

---

3. Which of the following figures will complete the given figure pattern?

 ___?___ 

A.  B.  C.  D. 

---

4. Which of the following letters is not present in the given figure?

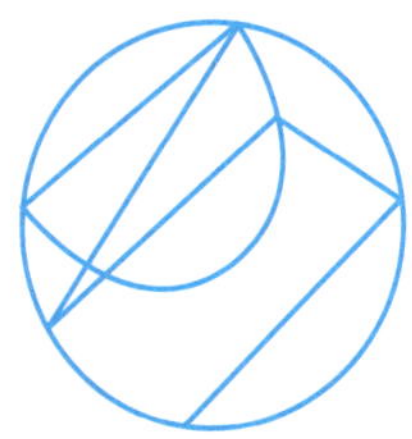

A. O
B. L
C. D
D. T

---

5. Cap ______ is third from the left end.

L S O P Q D T (Left)

A. T B. Q C. O D. S

SPACE FOR ROUGH WORK

6. 3 groups of ______ strawberries each can be formed from the given strawberries.

A. 5 B. 6 C. 7 D. 4

---

7. If Sun is called Moon, Moon is called Earth and Earth is called Star, then where does man live?

A. Sun B. Earth C. Star D. Moon

---

8. Which of the following options will complete the given figure pattern?

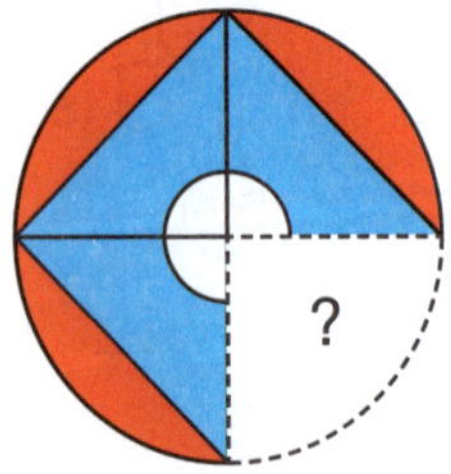

A. 

B. 

C. 

D. 

---

9. Arrange the given hockey sticks from largest to smallest.

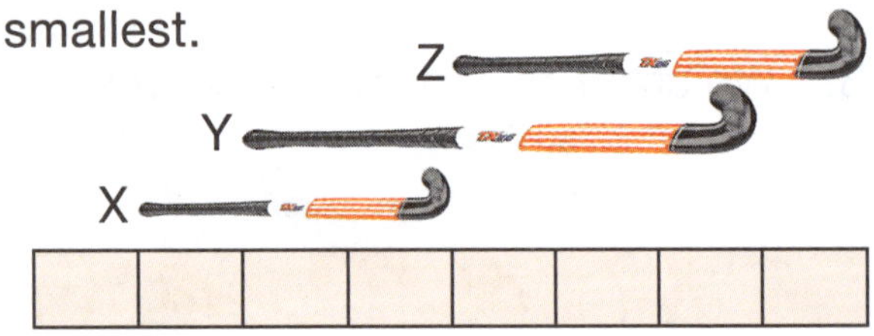

A. Y, X, Z
B. X, Y, Z
C. Y, Z, X
D. X, Z, Y

---

10. There are _________ slanting lines in the given figure.

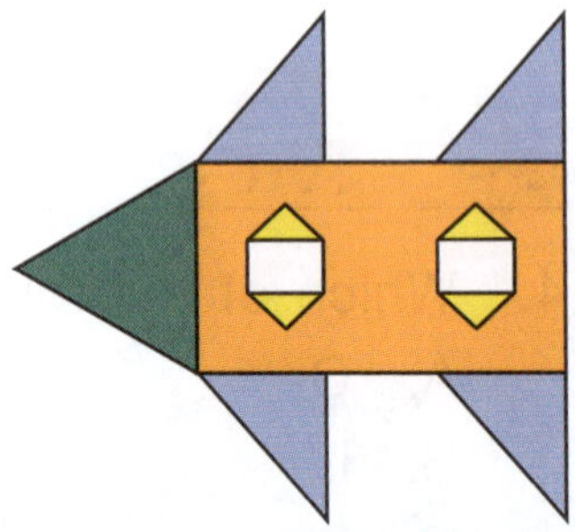

A. 14
B. 10
C. 12
D. 15

MATHEMATICAL REASONING

11. Which bear shows the largest value?

A. P
B. Q
C. R
D. S

SPACE FOR ROUGH WORK

12. Which of the following options represents the given number of parrots?

A. 1 tens less than 2 tens

B. 1 ones more than 2 tens

C. 1 ones less than 2 tens

D. 1 tens more than 1 ones

---

13. The given table shows the number of different types of trees in a garden. Find the total number of trees in the garden.

	Number of trees
Apple	112
Mango	120
Oak	210

A. 212

B. 442

C. 340

D. 368

---

14. Count the amount of money Raghu has.

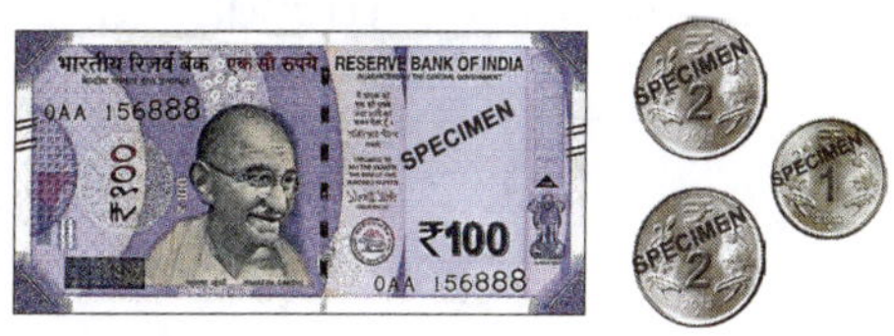

A. ₹ 102

B. ₹ 104

C. ₹ 100

D. ₹ 105

---

15. Study the given picture carefully.
The height of Kartik and Puneet together is ______ more than height of Kirti. (1 ⇧ = 1 unit)

A. 4 units

B. 3 units

C. 2 units

D. 5 units

---

16. What is the correct order from shortest to longest?

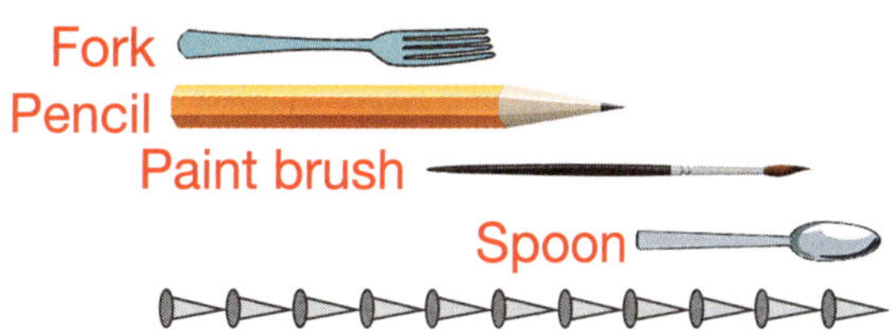

A. Pencil, Spoon, Fork, Paint brush

B. Pencil, Fork, Spoon, Paint brush

C. Spoon, Fork, Paint brush, Pencil

D. Spoon, Fork, Pencil, Paint brush

SPACE FOR ROUGH WORK

17. Which of the following looks like a cube?

A.  B.  C.  D. 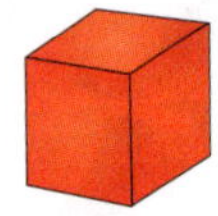

18. The total quantity of water in the given beakers is ________.

2 L 3 L 5 L 2 L

A. 10 L B. 8 L C. 12 L D. 11 L

Direction (19-20) : The given pictograph shows the number of food packets distributed by an NGO to the needy persons. Study it carefully and answer the following questions.

	Number of packets
Monday	
Tuesday	
Wednesday	
Thursday	
Friday	
Saturday	
Each  shows 50 packets.	

19. Total number of packets distributed on Monday, Tuesday and Thursday is __________.

A. 850 B. 800

C. 700 D. 400

20. On ________, the maximum number of food packets were distributed.

A. Saturday B. Wednesday

C. Monday D. Friday

EVERYDAY MATHEMATICS

21. A shopkeeper had 105 bulbs. Some of the bulbs were damaged and 70 good bulbs were left with him. How many bulbs were damaged?

A. 25 B. 35 C. 80 D. 75

22. There were 180 passengers in a train. On a station, 50 persons deboarded and 70 boarded the train. How many passengers are there in the train now?

A. 220 B. 130 C. 250 D. 200

23. Kiran is 44 kg heavier. Her brother is 2 kg lighter than Kiran. Find the total weight of Kiran and her brother.

A. 84 kg B. 86 kg C. 82 kg D. 85 kg

SPACE FOR ROUGH WORK

24. If the capacity of a jug is 2 L, then how many jugs are required to fill the given barrel?

A. 7

B. 8

C. 9

D. 5

18 litres

25. Priyanka asks Savita to tell the number on the given abacus. Which of the following could be the correct answer?

A. 420

B. 402

C. 204

D. 240

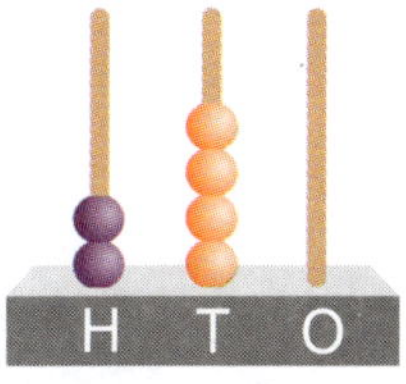

26. In a market, Kavya spent ₹ 180 on buying fruits, ₹ 310 on buying vegetables and ₹ 170 on grocery items. How much amount did she spend in all?

A. ₹ 550 B. ₹ 660 C. ₹ 610 D. ₹ 670

27. Varun saw the given painting in a shop.

How many triangles did Varun see?

A. 6

B. 7

C. 8

D. 10

28. Sahil saw two towers on a ground. Find the difference between the heights of the towers.

A. 17 m

B. 25 m

C. 35 m

D. 18 m

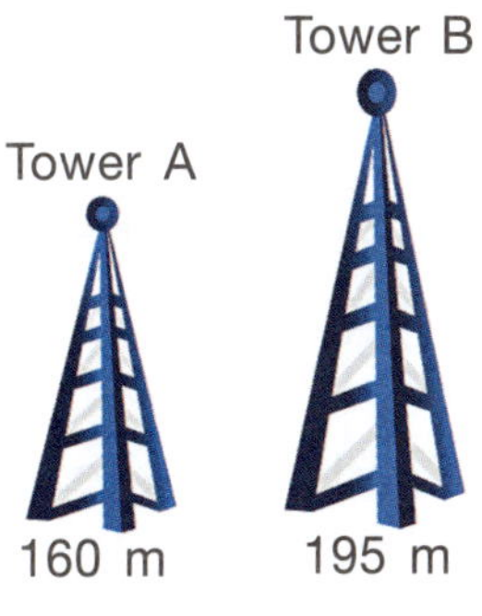

29. A school has 980 students. If 480 of them are boys, then how many girls are there in the school?

A. 400 B. 460 C. 500 D. 380

SPACE FOR ROUGH WORK

30. The number of seats in an auditorium is 715. Write the number name for the number of seats in the auditorium.

A. Seventy one hundred five
B. Seven hundred fifteen
C. Seven hundred fifty
D. Seven hundred fifty one

ACHIEVERS SECTION

31. Match the shapes in Column-2 which is drawn using the objects given in Column-1.

Column-1		**Column-2**	
(a)		(1)	
(b)		(2)	
(c)	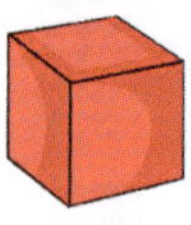	(3)	

	(a)	**(b)**	**(c)**
A.	(1)	(3)	(2)
B.	(2)	(3)	(1)
C.	(3)	(1)	(2)
D.	(2)	(1)	(3)

32. Four children hold the number chart.

Arrange the children in descending order according to their numbers.

A. R, S, Q, P
B. P, S, R, Q
C. P, Q, S, R
D. Q, R, S, P

33. Identify the 3-digit number.

- Its tens place digit is 5 more than its ones digit.
- Its hundreds place digit is the largest one digit even number.
- Its ones digit is 2.

A. 782
B. 762
C. 872
D. 278

SPACE FOR ROUGH WORK

34. Study the given figure carefully and answer the following questions.

Find the distance travelled by Aman, if he travelled from

(a) Home to School.

(b) Park to Market.

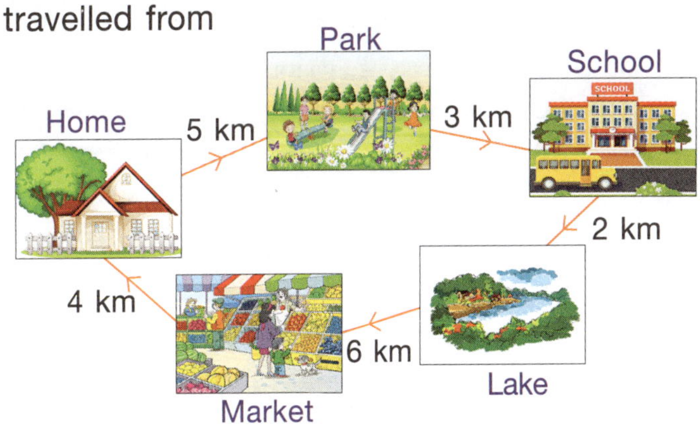

	(a)	(b)
A.	7 km	10 km
B.	8 km	10 km
C.	6 km	11 km
D.	8 km	11 km

---

35. Study the given figures carefully.

The weight of 3 bags is ________ .

A. 30 B. 10 C. 20 D. 15

ANSWER KEYS

1.	(B)	**2.**	(B)	**3.**	(A)	**4.**	(D)	**5.**	(B)	**6.**	(B)	**7.**	(C)
8.	(A)	**9.**	(C)	**10.**	(A)	**11.**	(C)	**12.**	(C)	**13.**	(B)	**14.**	(D)
15.	(C)	**16.**	(C)	**17.**	(D)	**18.**	(C)	**19.**	(A)	**20.**	(D)	**21.**	(B)
22.	(D)	**23.**	(B)	**24.**	(C)	**25.**	(D)	**26.**	(B)	**27.**	(B)	**28.**	(C)
29.	(C)	**30.**	(B)	**31.**	(B)	**32.**	(C)	**33.**	(C)	**34.**	(D)	**35.**	(A)

Answers

Chapter 1

Exercise 1A

1. a. 108, One hundred eight
   b. 161, One hundred sixty-one
2. a. 170 b. 187
3. a. One hundred forty-three
   b. One hundred fifty-five
4. a. 135 – One hundred thirty-five
   b. 103 – One hundred three
   c. 100 – One hundred
   d. 148 – One hundred forty-eight
   e. 176 – One hundred seventy-six
5.

151	152	153	154	155	156	157	158	159	160
161	**162**	163	164	165	166	167	168	**169**	170
171	172	173	174	**175**	**176**	177	178	179	180
181	182	183	184	185	186	187	188	189	**190**
191	192	193	**194**	195	196	**197**	198	199	**200**

6. a. 162 b. 197
7. a. 199 b. 126
8. 189, 188, 187, 186
9. 166 10. 111

Exercise 1B

1. a. Face Value – 7 Place Value – 7
   b. Face Value – 8 Place Value – 80
2. a. 100 + 50 + 0 b. 100 + 0 + 0
   c. 100 + 40 + 1 d. 100 + 10 + 3
3. a. 109 b. 167 c. 105 d. 123
4. a. 100 + 30 + 2 b. 100 + 10 + 5

Exercise 1C

1. a. 135 b. 200
   c. 111 d. 165
2. a. 111 b. 109
   c. 122 d. 116
3. a. 175 < 185 b. 146 > 144
   c. 198 < 200 d. 153 = 153
4. a. 194 b. 108
   c. 147 d. 195

Exercise 1D

1. a. 10, 110, 130, 155, 166, 190
   b. 45, 107, 111, 151, 170, 189
2. a. 200, 199, 198, 195, 192, 191
   b. 188, 181, 118, 110, 108, 106

Exercise 1E

1. a. first b. third c. fifth d. tie, fourth
   e. false f. second
2. a. B b. seventh c. J, I d. E, dark blue
   e. B, D, third

Exercise 1F

1. House A - 150, 142, 4, 160, 194
   House B - 125, 21, 161
2. b. 10, even c. 4, even
   d. 9, odd e. 3, odd
   f. 8, even
3. 

Chapter Revision

A. 1. 172, One hundred seventy-two
   2. 50 3. 1
B. 171, 172, 173, 174, 175, 176, 177, 178
C. 1. 109, 166, 175, 181, 190; 190, 181, 175, 166, 109
   2. 101, 110, 111, 114, 117; 117, 114, 111, 110, 101
D. 1. Ball 2. Tennis racket and ball
   3. sixth 4. fifth 5. fourth
E. Bag A – 200, 136, 140, 18, 192, 100, 62, 178
   Bag B – 49, 5, 165

Chapter 2

Exercise 2A

1. a. 8 b. 55 c. 83 d. 37
2. a. 5 b. 7 + 3 = 10 c. 3 + 4 = 7

Exercise 2B

1. a. 11 b. 94 c. 11 d. 81
2. a. 73 b. 90 c. 45 d. 84

Exercise 2C

1. a. 8 b. 9 c. 17 d. 16
2. a. 69 b. 97 c. 68 d. 96

Exercise 2D

a. 82 b. 40 c. 93 d. 95

Exercise 2E

1. 66 books
2. 93 samosas and pizzas
3. 84 pages
4. 85 pens
5. 68 bottles

Chapter Revision

A. 1. b. 2. b. 3. c.

B. 1. 50 + 30 = 8 tens
2. 20 + 21 + 35 = 35 + 21 + 20
3. 7 + 8 + 2 = 17
4. Ninety-five = 48 + 10 + 37
5. 1 + 29 = Thirty

C. 1. 64 2. 18 3. 84 4. 66

D. 1. 70 2. 70 3. 60 4. 1

E. 1. T 2. F 3. F

F. 1. 10 + 9 = 19 2. 94 marks

Chapter 3

Exercise 3A

1. 78 2. 35 3. 68 4. 34
5. 56 6. 18 7. 35 8. 35

Exercise 3B

1. 31 2. 82 3. 42

Exercise 3C

1. 21 2. 1
3. 22 toffees 4. 45 red cars
5. 11 pink roses 6. 15 chairs

Chapter Revision

A. 1. 36 2. 41 3. 50 4. 14

B. 45, Circle the numbers – 174, 89, 62, 158, 180

C. 1. 54 2. 13 3. 36 4. 42

D. 1. 31 2. 82

E. 1. F 2. F 3. F 4. T

F. 1. 88 2. 72 3. 16

G. 1. a. 48 balloons
b. 42 balloons
2. 53 monkeys
3. 24 children

Chapter 4

Exercise 4A

1. a. 4, 2, 1; Four hundred twenty-one
b. 3, 0, 7; Three hundred seven
c. 8, 3, 4; Eight hundred thirty-four
2. a. 9 hundreds 0 tens 6 ones, Nine hundred six
b. 2 hundreds 4 tens 3 ones, Two hundred forty-three
3. a. 431 b. 963 c. 619 d. 871

Exercise 4B

1. 323, 324, 326, 327, 328
2. 542, 543, 545, 546, 548, 549
3. 832, 833, 834, 836, 837, 839, 840
4. 672, 673, 674, 676, 677, 679

Exercise 4C

1. a. Place Value: 1 = 100 7 = 70 3 = 3
Face Value: 1 = 1 7 = 7 3 = 3
b. Place Value: 6 = 600 8 = 80 4 = 4
Face Value: 6 = 6 8 = 8 4 = 4
2. a. 3 hundreds 8 tens 5 ones, 300 + 80 + 5
b. 6 hundreds 9 tens 1 one, 600 + 90 + 1
3. a. 300 b. 70 c. 2
4. a. 4 b. 9 c. 6
5. a. 532 b. 7 c. 40 d. 900 + 9

Exercise 4D

1. a. 964 > 182 b. 729 > 607
c. 200 < 800 d. 521 < 906
e. 374 = 374 f. 189 > 183
2. a. 569 b. 843 c. 489
3. a. 478 b. 238 c. 341

Exercise 4E

1. a. 127, 349, 623, 805 b. 158, 673, 691, 908
2. a. 640, 573, 257, 189 b. 928, 746, 329, 150
3. a. 560, 570, 580, 590 b. 576, 676, 776, 876
c. 760, 750, 740, 730 d. 920, 910, 900, 890

Exercise 4F

1. a. 136 b. 624
c. 468 d. 855
2. a. 274 b. 497
c. 613 d. 800
3. a. 235 b. 722 c. 947 d. 670, 671

4. 446, 447

5. 868, 869, 870

Exercise 4G

1. 83, 38 2. 51, 15

3. 920, 209 4. 764, 467

Chapter Revision

A. 1. 4 hundreds, 3 tens, 8 ones, Four hundred thirty-eight

2. 2 hundreds 2 tens 8 ones, Two hundred twenty-eight

3. 999 4. 653 5. 930

6. 811, 812, 819, 821, 919

B. 623, 624, 626, 628, 629

C. 1. One hundred twenty-five

2. 100 + 20 + 5

3. Place Value = 20, Face Value = 2

D. 1. F 2. F 3. T

4. F 5. F

E. 1. 431 < 485 2. 221 > 212

3. 398 < 432 4. 817 < 877

F. 1. 710, 810, 910

2. 830, 840, 850, 870, 880

G. 456

H. 238, 239, 240 and 241

I. 985, 986, 987, 988 (All appropriate answers are accepted)

J. 211, Two hundred eleven

CHAPTER 5

Exercise 5A

1. a. 129 b. 120 c. 111 d. 125

2. 121 coins 3. 137 flowers

Exercise 5B

1. 179 2. 154 3. 198 4. 277

Exercise 5C

1. 967 2. 899 3. 973 4. 968

Exercise 5D

1. 272 2. 358 3. 556 4. 127

Exercise 5E

1. 368 people

2. 394 books

3. 479 ice creams

4. 698 marbles

Chapter Revision

A. 1. 83 2. 167

B. 1. 700 2. 10 + 245 = 255 3. 520

4. 133 5. 610, 710, 810

6. Three hundred fifty

C. 1. 746 2. 975 3. 47 4. 85

5. 658 6. 900

D. 1. 100 + 400 = Five hundred

2. 150 + 20 = One hundred seventy

3. 220 + 45 = Two hundred sixty-five

4. 350 + 130 = Four hundred eighty

E. 1. F 2. F 3. F 4. T

F. 1. 372 tables and chairs

2. 699 rose plants

3. 51 dolls

4. 568 students

CHAPTER 6

Exercise 6A

1. 985 2. 492

3. 811 4. 609

5. 261 6. 325

7. 352 8. 311

Exercise 6B

1. 511 2. 742

3. 528 4. 265

Exercise 6C

1. Col 1: 6; Col 2: 2; Col 3: 1
2. Col 1: 5; Col 2: 0; Col 3: 1
3. Col 1: 5; Col 2: 0; Col 3: 6
4. Col 1: 7; Col 2: 7; Col 3: 1
5. Col 1: 1; Col 2: 4; Col 3: 5
6. Col 1: 5; Col 2: 1; Col 3: 7
7. Col 1: 1; Col 2: 6; Col 3: 7
8. Col 1: 6; Col 2: 9; Col 3: 8

Exercise 6D

1. 144 seats

2. 251 apples

3. 373 marbles

4. 712 books

Chapter Revision

A. 1. 222 sweets 2. 441 3. 134

B. 1. 323 2. 343 3. 752 4. 260

C. 1. 357 – 150 = 207

2. 498 – 124 = 374

3. 873 – 53 = 820

D. 1.

	H	T	O
	6	5	4
–		4	4
	6	**1**	**0**

2.

	H	T	O
	8	4	3
–		4	0
	8	**0**	**3**

3.

	H	T	O
	6	3	5
–		3	1
	6	**0**	**4**

E. 1. 13 children 2. 110 biscuits

Chapter 7

Exercise 7A

1. a. 3 × 4 = 12 b. 4 × 3 = 12

2. a. 7 × 3 = 21 b. 4 × 7 = 28

c. 6 × 4 = 24 d. 3 × 9 = 27

3. a. 3 × 6 = 18 b. 4 × 8 = 32

c. 4 × 5 = 20 d. 9 × 3 = 27

Exercise 7B

2. a. 2 × 3 b. 2 × 5 c. 2 d. 16
e. 60 f. 25 g. 35 h. 0
i. 36 j. 0 k. 24 l. 32
m. 20 n. 20 o. 12

3. a. Multiplier – 2 Multiplicand – 5 Product – 10
b. Multiplier – 7 Multiplicand – 5 Product – 35

Exercise 7C

1. a. 10

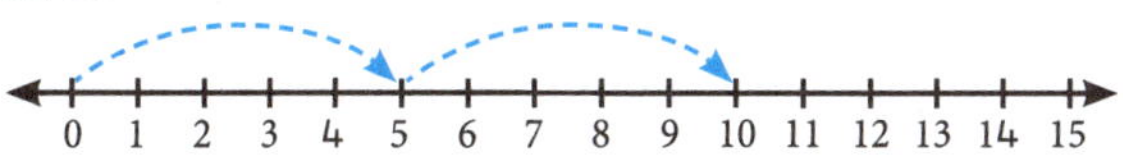

b. 12

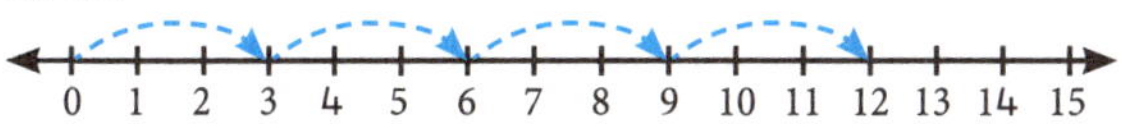

2. a. 14 b. 10 c. 52 d. 660

Exercise 7D

1. 45 2. 50 3. 56 4. 860

Exercise 7E

1. 32 2. 84 3. 96 4. 74 5. 90

Exercise 7F

1. Number of children in 1 row = 6
Number of children in 3 rows = 3 × 6 = 18 children

2. Number of pieces in 1 packet = 9
Number of pieces in 5 packets = 5 × 9 = 45 pieces of cookies

3. Number of shirts sold in 1 month = 323
Number of shirts sold in 2 months
= 2 × 323 = 646 shirts

4. Number of people in 1 train = 230
Number of people in 3 trains = 3 × 230 = 690 people

5. Cost of 1 box of erasers = 45
Cost of 6 boxes of erasers = 6 × 45 = ₹270

Chapter Revision

A.

	Multiplier	Multiplicand	Product
1.	6	7	42
2.	0	10	0
3.	1	9	9
4.	5	5	25

B. 1. c. 2. a. 3. b. 4. d.

C. 1. 8, 12, 20 2. 14, 28 3. 6, 9
4. 27, 36, 45

D. 1. 24 2. 0, 2, 4, 6 3. 0 and 5 4. 0

E. 1. 60 2. 200 3. 8 4. 15
5. 40 6. 9 7. 0 8. 60

F. 1. 32 sandwiches 2. ₹360 3. 80 people

Chapter 8

Exercise 8A

1. 3 2. 3 3. 4 4. 2 5. 3

Exercise 8B

1. a. 10 b. 6 c. 7 d. 4

2. a. 12 ÷ 4 b. 10 ÷ 5 3. a. 6

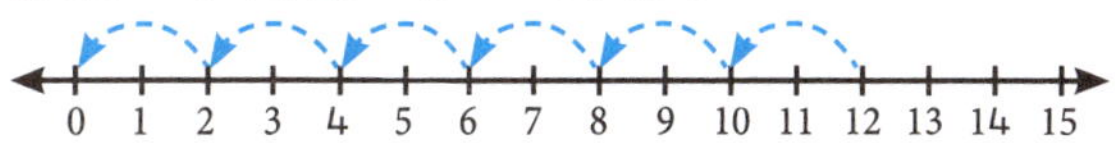

b. 5

Chapter Revision

A. 1. 3 2. 2 3. 5 4. 4 5. 2, 5

B. 1. T 2. T
3. a. F b. T 4. F
5. T 6. F

C. 1. 2 pages 2. 2 apples 3. 7 packets

CHAPTER 9

Exercise 9A

1. metre 2. b., d. 3. b., c., d.

4. a. m b. cm c. m d. m

Exercise 9B

1. a. 2 kg b. 10 g c. 5 g d. 100 g

2. 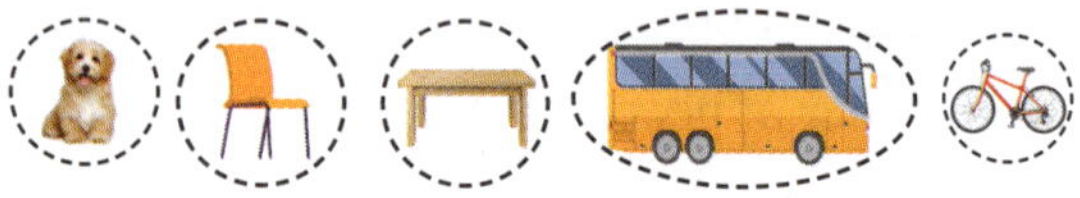

3. a. 1 kg b. 500 g c. 250 g d. 100 g

Exercise 9C

1. a. 5 mℓ b. 1 mℓ c. 250 mℓ d. 20 ℓ

2. Tick (✓) – a., b., d., e. Cross (✗) – c.

Chapter Revision

A. 1. 2 m 2. 15 cm

B. 1. 100 g 2. 15 kg

C. 1. 20 mℓ 2. 5 ℓ

D. 1. m, cm 2. cm 3. g, kg 4. g 5. ℓ

E. 1. longer 2. lighter 3. greater

CHAPTER 10

Exercise 10A

A. 1. Cloud – C
2. Design on the roof – C
3. Road towards the house – C
4. Rays of the sun – S
5. Side of the door – H
6. Tree trunk – V

Exercise 10B

1. 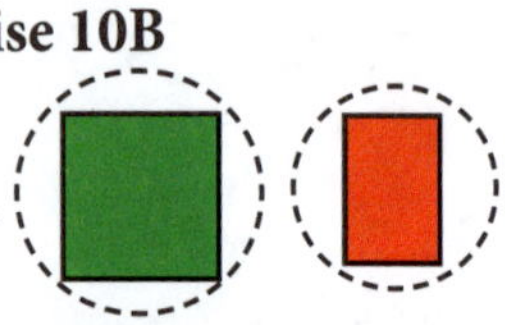 2. 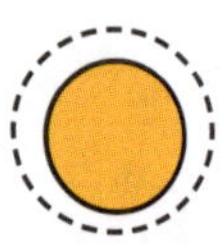

Exercise 10C

1. Globe – Red, Candle – Green, Book – Pink, Pencil Box – Pink, Carton box – Pink, Ball – Red, Pizza slice – Purple, Opened box shown to the right of the ball – Pink, Lamp – Green, Sofa – Blue

2. Food packet – Cuboid
Cell – Cylinder
Eraser – Cuboid
Tissue roll – Cylinder
Water bubbles – Sphere
Balloon – Sphere

3. a. S b. R c. S d. RS
e. RS f. RS g. S
h. S i. RS

Exercise 10D

1.  2.  3. 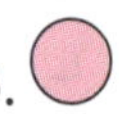 4. 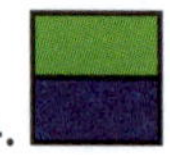

5. 8, 12, 16 6. 14, 16, 18; 2

Chapter Revision

B. 1. F 2. T 3. F 4. T 5. T

C. 1. Cuboid 2. Cube
3. Cylinder 4. Cone
5. Cuboid 6. Sphere

D. 1. 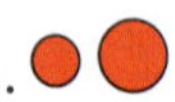 2.  3. B, A
4. X, Y, Z 5. 60, 50, 40; 10

CHAPTER 11

Exercise 11A

1. a. ₹60 b. ₹72 c. ₹201 d. ₹600

2. a. < b. > c. = d. >

Exercise 11B

1. ₹790 2. ₹120 3. ₹20
4. ₹880

Chapter Revision

A. 1. < 2. >

B. 1. ₹620 2. ₹16

C. 1. ₹750 2. ₹460 3. ₹214

4. ₹62, combination of notes and coins is ₹50 note, ₹10 note and ₹2 coin.

CHAPTER 12

Exercise 12A

1. a. 1:30 b. 7:30 c. 9:30 d. 3:30

2. a. 

b. 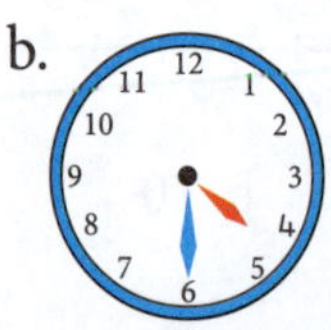

c.

d.

3. a. 8:30 b. 9:00 c. 11:30 d. 1:00, 1:30
   e. 2:30

Exercise 12B

1. a. Seven b. Wednesday c. Saturday
   d. Tuesday e. Friday
2. a. Sunday b. Tuesday c. Thursday
   d. Sunday
3. Wednesday

Exercise 12C

1. a. March b. July c. February
   d. November e. June
2. a. April, June, September, November
   d. autumn e. summer f. winter g. pleasant
   h. monsoon (rainy)
3. a. Summer b. Autumn c. Winter
   d. Spring e. Monsoon (Rainy)

Chapter Revision

A. 1. 11:30 2. 7 3. Friday 4. Spring

B. 1.

2.

3.

4.

C. 1. F 2. T 3. F 4. F 5. F

D. 1. January, May, August, October
   2. Friday 3. May 4. Sunday

CHAPTER 13

Exercise 13A

1. a. Pencils – 7, Erasers – 6,
   Pens – 5, Rulers – 4, Notebooks – 3
   b. 25 items c. 4 pencils
   d. Pencils e. Notebooks f. 3
2. a. Red – 4, Yellow – 5, Blue – 2, Green – 2
   b. 13 c. 4 d. 8
   e. 8 cubes and 2 cuboids, that is, 10
   f. greater

Chapter Revision

A. 1. 2 dresses 2. 6 pens 3. 5 pens
   4. 1 book 5. 2 pairs

B. 1. Monday – 3, Tuesday – 2, Wednesday – 3, Thursday – 4, Friday – 5, Saturday – 6, Sunday – 7
   2. 30
   3. 2
   4. Tuesday
   5. Sunday
   6. Monday and Wednesday

SEE Social Emotional Ethical Learning

21 CS Collaboration, Communication

CC Integration with Environmental Studies

HQ Coexisting with Nature

Do Not Litter, Keep It Clean!

My SEE (Social Emotional Ethical) Space

A. **Answer the following questions.**

1. What was the total number of pieces of litter picked up by Class 2A students?

   ____

2. Which class picked up the least number of pieces of litter?

   ____

3. What was the total number of pieces of litter picked up by all students?

   ____

4. How many students were there for the clean-up day?

   ____

B. **Why do you think we should keep our surroundings clean? Share your thoughts in the space given below.**

____

____

C. **If a class can collect this amount of litter, imagine how much litter can be collected by the whole world! Also, why is keeping your surroundings clean important? Write down some important points.**

Maths Mela

21 CS Creativity and Innovation | EL | AI

Let us build a multiplication table wheel for number 5.

All you need is... Chart papers of different colours, a pair of scissors, a shirt button and a thin wire

Note:
Do not use scissors or cutter yourself. Take help of an elder while cutting.

Let's Start!

1. Take a yellow chart. Place a medium-sized plate over it and trace its outline.

2. Similarly, trace the outline of the plate on an orange chart.

3. 

Now, take a small bowl and trace its outline on a blue chart.

4. Take the cutouts of all circles. Now, mark their centres.

5. Place the circles one over the other as shown and make a hole in the centre of all circles with a pencil.

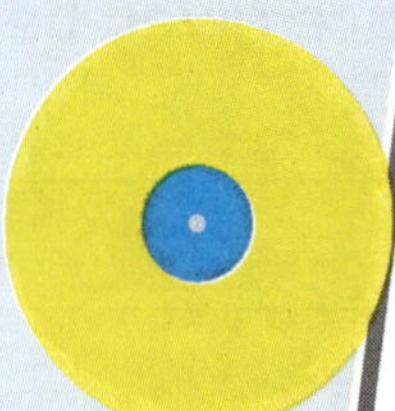

6. 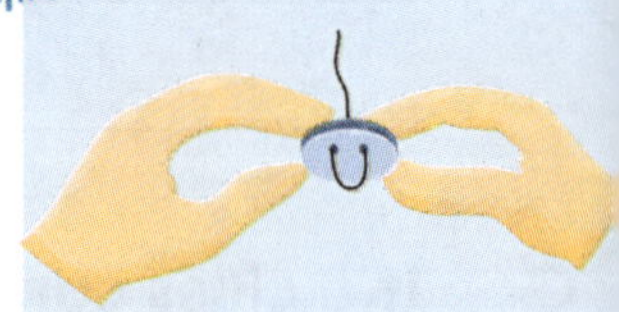

Take a shirt button and pass a thin wire from it to the centre of the circles.

7. Open both the ends of the wire from the opposite side.

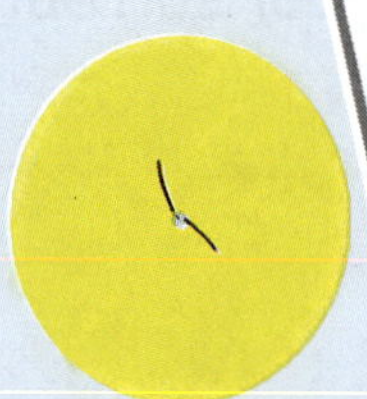

8. Cut two shapes from the yellow circle as shown.

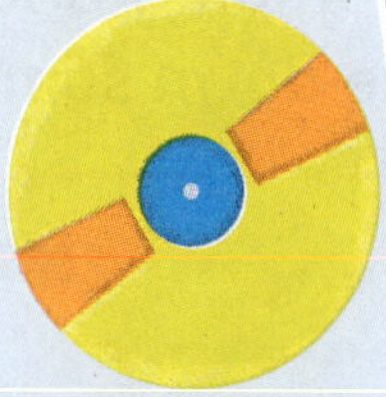

9. 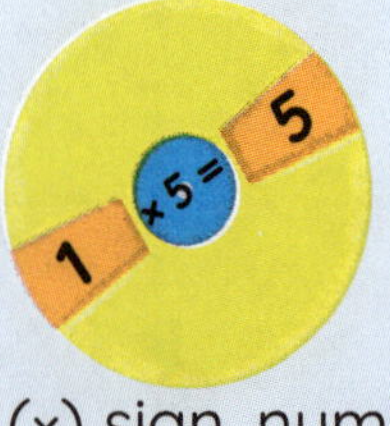

Write 1 in the first shape, followed with multiplication (×) sign, number 5 and equals to (=) sign in the smallest circle. Now, write 5 in the other shape.

10. 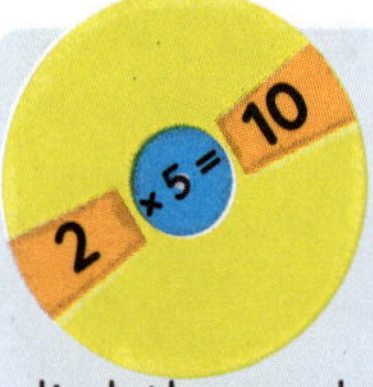

Rotate the yellow circle slightly and write 2 in the first and 10 in the second shape. Repeat this step till whole orange circle is filled with numbers.

11. Rotate the yellow circle and justify the multiplication table of 5.

Do It Yourself!

Can you make a model from cardboard for the addition of two 1-digit numbers? Give a brief idea about the model in the space given below.

Create a maths model for addition. Write the materials required and the steps of its construction. Draw a picture of your model in the space given below.

All I Need Is:

Let's Start:

Eminent Mathematicians

RADHANATH SIKDAR
(OCTOBER 1813–17 MAY 1870)

He was an Indian Bengali mathematician, who is best known for finding the height of Mount Everest.

JOHANN RAHN
(10 MARCH 1622–25 MAY 1676)

He was a Swiss mathematician, who is known to be the first user of the division symbol (÷) and the therefore sign (∴).

THOMAS HARRIOT
(C. 1560–2 JULY 1621)

He was an English astronomer, mathematician and translator. He is known for introducing symbols for 'is less than (<)' and 'is greater than (>)'.

ROBERT RECORDE
(C. 1512–1558)

He was a Welsh physician and mathematician. He invented the equals sign (=).

MARYAM MIRZAKHANI
(12 MAY 1977–14 JULY 2017)

She was born in Iran. She became the first Iranian student to achieve a perfect score in the International Mathematical Olympiad during her teenage years. She won two gold medals. She was the first female who received the Fields Medal in 2014, the most prestigious award in mathematics. She was a mathematics professor at Stanford University in the U.S. She is considered as one of the greatest mathematicians of recent times.